PICKING UP THE PIECES

PICKING UP THE PIECES

Reshaping a Life Torn by Divorce

Patricia Chavez
and
Clif Cartland

THOMAS NELSON PUBLISHERS
Nashville

 Published in Nashville, Tennessee, by Thomas Nelson Inc., Publishers, and simultaneously in Don Mills, Ontario, by Thomas Nelson & Sons (Canada) Limited. Manufactured in the United States of America.

Library of Congress Cataloging in Publication Data

Chavez, Patricia.
Picking up the pieces.

1. Chavez, Patricia. 2. Divorcees—United States—Biography. 3. Christian-life—1960-
I. Cartland, Clif, joint author. II. Title.
HQ834.C54 301.42'84'0924 79-19377
ISBN 0-8407-5162-7

CONTENTS

PART I

DETOURS ON THE ROAD TO HAPPILY EVER AFTER: AN HONEST LOOK AT THE WORLD OF THE SUDDENLY SINGLE

PART II

PITFALLS AND POSSIBILITIES: A PRACTICAL GUIDE TO LIFE AFTER DIVORCE

To Faith, my wife of twenty-five years, and to our children: Paul, Jeannette, and Jennifer, whose love and support made this writing possible.

To Pat, who shared her story so openly and honestly . . . so that others might pick up the pieces.

To all the storytellers who have warmed my heart and made love their art. And to the faithful editors at Thomas Nelson who helped refine this story.

In deep gratitude to God for his gifts and his faithfulness.

—Clif Cartland

PART I

DETOURS ON THE ROAD TO HAPPILY EVER AFTER

CHAPTER 1

Earth-tone Vessels

Many years ago the English Duke of Portland owned a magnificent vase, a truly brilliant work of art. The Portland Vase, as it was called, was its owner's prized possession.

As he admired it one day, a thought came to the duke's mind. "Beauty such as this should be shared with the world. I want to loan the Portland Vase to the British Museum for everyone to enjoy."

The vase was soon prominently displayed at the museum, and the immediate public acclaim of the vase gave the duke a great sense of satisfaction.

Shortly after the opening of the display, the duke found it necessary to dismiss one of his most trusted employees. The servant was so deeply hurt by this that he sought some means of revenge, some way to bring pain to the duke.

Then he thought of the vase. Overnight, he traveled to London and paid the few pennies admission to see the vase. Planning his moves very carefully, he waited until there were no other visitors in the display room and the eyes of the guard were turned away. Carefully he crept under the protective ropes, picked up the vase, and dashed it to the ground.

The servant was quickly captured by the guards, and shocked museum officials sealed off the display room, leaving the broken pieces strewn across the floor.

When the duke was told what had happened, he immediately ordered that none of the pieces be touched. Even the tiniest chips were to be left where they had dropped. Then in Stoke-on-Trent, the pottery capital of England, the duke searched for someone who would attempt to put the vase back together again. One craftsman after another turned him down. Everywhere he went he was told that the job could not be done.

The duke was close to abandoning his search when he went to one last shop and told his story one last time. To his surprise, this craftsman agreed to try the restoration.

"But why are you willing to try?" the duke inquired. "Everyone else has turned me down. I can't understand."

"Your Lordship, my father made the Portland Vase. The pieces on the museum floor are all that is left of his finest work. I must try to rebuild my father's masterpiece."

And so, working at the museum day after weary day, the craftsman added a piece here and a sliver there. At times he despaired that the job would ever be done. Then, finally, he was finished.

The duke was overjoyed at the results. "It is a masterpiece," he exclaimed. "A second masterpiece, more beautiful now than it was before."

Once more the great vase was put on display. And once more the doors to the display room were thrown open so that the world could see the great vase.

EARTH-TONE VESSELS

* * *

The story you are about to read is the story of one woman's divorce and her attempt to pick up the pieces of her life. Although the story is true, some names have been changed to provide confidentiality. These are real people in real situations, telling a story that needs to be told.

You'll find the full range of emotions in this story, and if I have done my work well you will do more than read about those emotions. You will experience them. You'll find yourself liking some of the people and disliking others. You'll wonder why he or she could be so dumb as to miss what was really happening.

The very human portraits you are about to see have been drawn in earth tones. When the people in this story are angry, they are *really* angry. When their thoughts or actions are inconsistent, I have not tried to make them consistent. That would only have robbed the story of much of its strength and distorted the portrait.

I wish the story could have been told in reverse, bringing the brighter days of recovery nearer to the beginning. But that, too, would have distorted things. The sun of recovery that warms the final chapters must be seen in contrast to the cold, painful night of the early chapters. As you relive something of that night, I trust that the darkest splashes on this human canvas will sober you and, at the same time, help you to more fully appreciate the bright touches when they come.

I do not celebrate divorce in the pages ahead. This is a painfully human story of two once-lovers whose relationship darkens and then divides. Even the recovery process is a difficult one. Picking up the pieces is a traumatic experience.

Woven throughout the drama of this story there *is* celebration, a celebration of life and a rousing symphony of hope. Perhaps more than anything else, this story is a statement about the possibility of new life in the midst of despair. It is my way of saying, "Don't give up. Life is not over."

* * *

Part 1 of this book—"Detours on the Road to Happily Ever After"—is a very personal story that allows you to walk freely across the landscape of another human life, feeling the warmth of intimacy and the depths of despair.

A stimulating road map to recovery follows in Part 2—"Pitfalls and Possibilities." Born of my experience and seasoned by my hundreds of hours counseling both those on the verge of divorce and those who have taken that step, these chapters are intensely practical.

You will find suggestions on how to handle the legal process, what to do about meals, and how to cope with the empty bed. You'll look at recovery stages, how to start living again, how to deal with anger, and how to discover ways to know what you really want out of life. I explore relationships with an ex-mate, the children, and friends. I'll talk frankly about dating and sex.

This is not a cold textbook. Most suggestions are illustrated from real life. If I think the answer I offer is really the *only* answer, I say so. But most of the time I'm giving you one of many possible answers—my answer, born out of my experience.

Never in my wildest dreams would I expect you to agree with everything I suggest. But if what I say raises questions and provokes dialogue, I will be grateful.

Remember: The pain and the stark reality of this story

does in the end give way to a new day and a fresh wind that blows away the murky remains of a hard-to-forget past. Keep that bright hope in mind as this story unfolds.

But more than anything else, keep that good news in mind as *your* personal story unfolds.

CHAPTER 2

Saturday Night Live

It was early Sunday morning. And it was my thirtieth birthday. Our two girls, Karen, 9, and Jennifer, 7, had stayed overnight with friends.

Our house was still, with a silence that was more than the absence of children's voices. It was that painful, intense stillness that can only be created by two people who have decided not to talk to each other—the awful stillness of bitter words unspoken, yet rumbling just below the surface. It was the cold, tense silence that comes before the storm.

Like almost every morning of our twelve years of marriage, I made a pot of coffee. It was one of those little daily rituals that, even in times of tension, make it seem as if life is going on unchanged.

Mechanically, I took two cups from the cupboard and sat at the breakfast nook, feeling numb on the inside and waiting for the coffee to brew.

Allen came into the kitchen, poured the coffee, and carried it into the living room. He didn't ask me to join him; he simply expected that I would follow. And I did.

We sat across from each other. At first there was an awkward silence, and then the words that had been below the surface began to tumble out. But the storm I had expected wasn't there. Instead, Allen was the very soul of quiet, clear logic.

"This just isn't going to work for us," he said. "We've tried, and it just isn't working. Last night was the final blow, Pat."

Last night!

I felt a painful kind of relief. Finally we were going to talk about last night. At least, Allen was going to talk about it. I was still silent, just listening and reflecting.

Last night. My mind went back. It had begun so innocently—three couples getting together to celebrate my birthday. Boy, did I need to celebrate. Something! Anything! A birthday was a great excuse.

On the surface, my life looked like a young woman's dream: a good husband—a doctor of veterinary medicine—two beautiful daughters, and a pretty house in San Francisco. A real dream. But underneath, I had just begun to admit the feeling that we held all of this together only for convenience—*Allen's* convenience. It had been a long, long time since he had showed any interest in me at all as a woman. I had the nagging feeling that Allen was *stuck* with me. I was the mother of his children and that was all. Our relationship—what was left of it—was empty.

Oh, how I wanted our relationship to be something more. I wanted it to be richer, fuller. I wanted it to be all the good things you read about in *Good Housekeeping* and *Woman's Day*. But I didn't know how to communicate that to Allen. I didn't know how to put what I was feeling into words he would hear . . . and do something about.

As I sat in the living room that morning, I felt a deep sense of emptiness . . . dissatisfaction . . . hurt. I felt that if I were ever to please Allen, I would have to measure up to something, but I didn't know what.

Allen had always talked about how our backgrounds were different, meaning that his was wonderful and mine was not so good. He had loving, caring parents and a stable home. I was constantly reminded that my father was "an alcoholic," a military officer who was "rootless, who traveled from one end of the world to the other." My stepmother was a "pathological liar." All of that was *true*, but the way Allen said it made me feel worthless.

Before we were married, Allen talked of taking me out of "that situation." I was going to be rescued by my lover. But within just a year after we were married, all that began to change. It was no longer "that situation." He began to talk about having made "a mistake."

"If I'd really been honest about it," he would say, "I should have realized from the beginning that our backgrounds were so different that this just wasn't going to work."

Every time we had an argument his response was the same. "Of course, I couldn't expect anything else. We're so different."

Recently the bickering about our "different backgrounds" had taken a new, more painful direction. Allen was beyond the comparison stage. Now he was saying, "There's no point in attempting to make anything out of this relationship. Just be the mother of my kids, Pat. That's all there is left."

Last night. The words echoed again in the emptiness that gripped me. And that sound brought me back to thoughts of the birthday party. One of the men at the party—a good-looking military man—had seemed attracted to me. Actually, there was no "seemed" about it; it was obvious. Somehow it gave me a glimmer of hope; I was attractive to someone. *He* didn't care about my "different background."

I drank up his attention and held out my cup for more. I remember feeling that I wasn't all that attracted to him, but I quickly dismissed that thought. He was coming on strong, and I loved every moment of it. All evening long my actions were crying out, "Look at me, Allen! Look at what's happening. Somebody finds me attractive!"

I had never been more than an occasional drinker. But that night I drank too much. I remember it well, because I was doing it deliberately. It was the only way I could think of to get back at Allen. I thought I was punishing him somehow. Deep inside I hated what I was doing, and I hated myself for doing it. Yet it almost seemed like a deliberate, calculated move.

"You think I'm so bad," my actions screamed. "Well, I'll show you how bad I *really* am." My feelings were confused. I wanted so much for Allen to love me. I really loved him in spite of everything. Yet I was deliberately doing things that would turn him away—incredible, bizarre kinds of things. In front of everyone, I was proving to him that I was exactly what he thought I was.

In one short evening an innocent friendship became a flaming seduction. My military man took me off to the bedroom for the final stages of this intimate battle, and the "enemy" offered no resistance.

It was almost as if there were two Pats there that evening. The real me—the me that wanted so much to be loved—was watching this other woman throw away the only love she knew. Allen broke in on us with the curt announcement that he was taking me home. I went with him in silence, feeling guilty and beaten.

I wanted him to say, "Listen! You are my wife. You belong to me. We are not going to have another night like this. I love you. From now on you will behave!"

I'd have given anything if he had said, "Pat, you're reaching out for something I haven't been giving you. I love you . . . and I'm sorry."

But he didn't. Knowing Allen, he couldn't. That was too much to expect.

During the ride home, he broke the silence only to say, "If you love that guy, do whatever you want to do. This has never been much of a relationship anyway."

Never? I thought to myself. *Never?*

There *had* been good times along with the bad. But that night I knew it was all gone. I'd blown the marriage. I felt confused, dirty, and unworthy.

I had felt that Allen simply didn't care any more, and that fear had made me panic. I had reached out to someone who seemed to say I was attractive. In a logic distorted by fear, I had hoped that the realization that someone else cared about me would be a shock to Allen, a shock that would bring him running back to me.

But it hadn't worked.

Now, sitting in the living room in the harsh reality of Sunday morning, my feelings of unworthiness were compounded by the hopelessness I felt in the pit of my stomach. "Last night," I heard Allen say. His voice brought me back to the raw reality of the moment.

As he talked, I remember feeling, *It's over!* His voice was calm. He wasn't angry or malicious. I think I could have responded to anger. Instead, it was almost as if he were a newscaster reporting some event half a world away. There was no emotion.

In a cold, calculated way he said, "I'm not surprised that we've ended up this way. I've been expecting something like this."

Inside I felt a crazy mixture of feelings. Part of me was saying, "You're guilty, Pat. Face it squarely and honestly. For once in your life don't rationalize or make excuses."

Yet amidst the guilt, frustration, and hopelessness, another voice was saying, "No. No. No. Wait a minute. This isn't *all* your fault. There's another side to the story. There is *some* good in you. There has to be."

"It's more than I can take, Pat." There was a note of finality in his voice. Then calmly he added, "I want you to give me a divorce."

There it was. That dreaded word was out in the open. Somehow I had known it was coming.

"Of course," I agreed. There was no reason to fight back, no will to argue. I was resigned to the inevitable.

I could feel the pain, the absolute frustration of knowing that I could not say a single word that would make any difference. There wasn't even a way to let my feelings out. Somewhere in the long-ago past I had made a conscious decision to mask my feelings, and I couldn't change now even if I wanted to.

With my marriage breaking up, I was able to look Allen right in the eye and not show my feelings. It was almost as if I had consciously decided, "I'll die before I let you see how much I hurt." And I succeeded, almost to the point of fooling myself about the real depth of my feelings.

Allen talked about how he had tried to make the marriage work. I wanted to scream out, "Who are you kidding? You didn't try anything but to get what you needed and wanted out of me." But I didn't respond. Instead, I slipped back into my bitter memories.

During much of our marriage I had felt used. Ten of those years I had worked to support the family while Allen went to school. When he was in veterinary school in Colorado State I had worked especially hard—fifty to sixty hours a week. We had one of the best-looking student apartments . . . on next to nothing. Even though I was the highest-paid student wife on campus, every penny went toward Allen's schooling. We couldn't buy furniture, so I bought corduroy and reupholstered old things. I learned to put cornmeal in paint to make cracked walls look like they've had a new coat of rough plaster.

I had done every bit of that willingly. But Allen's attitude had always seemed to be, "That's what you're *supposed* to do as my wife. If you want all the pie-in-the-sky-by-and-by when we graduate, you're supposed to work."

Finally we had reached a point in our lives when the pressures to put Allen through school were over. He had graduated. It felt like "we" had graduated. I'd worked at it just like he had. Now I deserved to stay home and be a wife and mother.

That's what I wanted to do. But already Allen had begun to put pressure on me to go back to work and earn more money.

"What I'm making isn't enough," he would say over and over again.

And my insides responded, "Wait a minute! That wasn't in the bargain. The agreement was that I would work for you and then you would work for me. Now you don't want to do that. You want *me* to work for me."

In the living room, sipping our coffee, I wanted to scream at Allen. I wanted to pour out all my feelings, all my frustrations. I wanted to make him face all the pain I had experienced. I wanted to bury that one brief Saturday night affair under an avalanche of my hurts. Maybe if I had been able to, it would have stopped Allen short . . . maybe.

But I couldn't.

Instead, I meekly agreed to leave that day. "Yes, you can have your divorce." It was as if we were making some kind of business deal.

It was time to pick up the girls. They had been at a birthday party and then stayed overnight at a friend's house. We went together in the car. On the way home, we went through the "Did you have a good time?" routine. "Yes, it was fun." Life was always fun for little girls.

"What was your party like?" they asked me.

"Oh, it was fine," I lied. At a time like that you hold up a facade for all to see, don't you?

In the back seat of the car the girls were yelling and shouting. To them the world was a warm, exciting place. Only a few feet away in the front seat, everything was cold. In spite of the bright sunshine of the day, I felt a creeping, paralyzing cold.

I was carefully shutting down my emotions. I could feel it happening. "Don't let anyone see what you're feeling . . . or even thinking," I told myself.

Back in the house, Allen called Jennifer and Karen, "Come here, kids. We have something to talk about." I saw fear come across their faces as we sat down. Then, quietly, Allen explained that Mother and Daddy wouldn't be living together any more.

I can remember the girls crying. That's a vivid, painful memory. I can remember trying not to feel their hurt *or* my own.

Through their tears, Allen explained that I would be leaving. Of course, they would see me after the divorce. I would be talking to them and they could write me. What empty platitudes to lighten the hurt of little hearts!

I listened, and it seemed as if we were going through the steps of a mathematical formula. We were coldly and logically disbanding our marriage and our family. Methodically, we were arranging for the proper care and disposition of each piece.

We had already decided that the children would remain there in the house. *Of course.* It was going to be hard enough on them as it was. There was no reason to pull them out of school in the middle of the year. Allen would make arrangements for a housekeeper for them, while I went to Las Vegas to take care of the divorce.

In just a few weeks, when it was all over, we'd make other arrangements and then we would all get down to the task of living our new lives.

It was almost over. I watched the girls as their world broke in pieces. I held them. And out of my pain, I tried to offer comfort. But I didn't really have any to give.

In a moment like that, you can only cling to each other and trust the deep, unspoken emotions of the heart to speak their message. Mother and daughters, holding each other tightly, knowing their lives would never be the same again.

Looking back on that moment, I've wondered what would have happened if I had said to Allen, "I understand what you're saying. I blew it. Maybe we can't live together any more. But I'm not moving anyplace. The divorce is *your* idea. You do whatever you want to do. *You* move out. *You* go to Las Vegas. The girls and I are going to stay here."

Instead, I accepted the role of the bad guy. I deserved to be kicked out.

Silently I went to the bedroom, packed a few things, threw them in my car, and *got out of there.* I decided to head for the only rock I knew in this storm—the home of my uncle and aunt.

CHAPTER 3

The Still Before the Storm

On the freeway headed south, some inner chauffeur must have driven the car. Lost in a flood of memories, I thought back to earlier, happier days.

I could see my brown-skinned, grey-haired grandmother standing at the old woodburning stove. She was short and chubby, all soft and warm and smelling like the good, clean smell of tortillas.

I was just a little girl then, and Grandmother seemed very, very old. In fact, she was only in her early forties. She had married when she was thirteen. My father, the oldest of ten children, had been born when she was just fifteen.

Grandmother was "Mommy" to me. My mother had died when I was born, and my father had left shortly after that. My grandparents became my parents, and they loved me in a million ways.

Home was a simple place. In my mind's eye it was still easy to recapture the little village of Los Lunas, New Mexico. Our brick house stood out among the adobe homes. I could see Grandmother on her hands and knees, scrubbing the wood floor with lye until it was grey-white. And I remembered how important it was to her to try to make flowers grow in the desert sand. I smiled as I thought of the time she had two trees cut down in the front yard. "Flowers will grow well around the rotting stumps," she explained. And they did!

Grandfather always seemed to be looking for work. There were many mouths to feed. I could always tell when it was pay day because he would come home with a little brown paper sack full of candy for me.

He saved every penny he could to buy me a Shetland pony. It was very small and mangy, but Toby was *mine*.

I remembered happy times at our house when my uncles played guitars and mandolins, and everybody danced and drank wine, and I drained the wine glasses. I thought we were rich. In a way we were—rich in love.

In those early years it was hard for me to remember my father. He was like a fairy tale character to me. My uncles adored him and told me stories about him. He was the family hero. When he came home he wore an army uniform (he was an officer), and everybody paid a lot of attention to him. I remember that. But it was always hard for me to think of him as Daddy. "Daddy" was the man who lived there and brought me candy. "Daddy" was my grandfather.

One day after school, in the winter before my ninth birthday, Grandmother sat me down and explained that my dad and my stepmother were coming to get me and that I was going to live with them. She told me all the wonderful things they would do for me that she could not do. I would travel. I would have nice clothes and a nicer place to live.

Then she added, "I want you to be a good girl." I remembered those words clearly. Many years later I was still trying to "be a good girl" for Grandmother.

I traveled across the country with my parents, but we didn't stay anyplace very long. He was always being transferred to another base. Each year my father would accumulate enough leave so that he could go deer hunting in Jerome, Arizona, in the fall. While Dad hunted, I was enrolled briefly in school in Jerome. That's where I first met Allen.

Football player . . . basketball player . . . high-school hero . . . son of a successful cattle rancher . . . product of one of Jerome's leading families—that was Allen. He was good-looking and out of my reach. I knew who he was, but that was all. We never met.

When Dad's leave was over we moved back to Salt Lake City, where he was to be stationed. I was planning to be a nurse, and Salt Lake City's Holy Cross Hospital had a good school of nursing. In my junior year in high school I worked at the hospital as a nurses' aide. I thought that would increase my chances of being accepted into nursing school.

It worked. I was accepted. My young life was beginning to fit together. The pieces were falling into place. High-school graduation was followed by those wonderful, carefree, lazy days of summer. And then came the planning for nursing school. Those were the years of the Korean War, and that summer Dad received his orders to report for duty in Korea. So my stepmother and I packed up and moved back to Jerome to stay with my stepmother's brother. I didn't mind the move or Dad's absence. I would be leaving soon anyway. It was almost time for school.

Then, just two weeks before I was scheduled to return to Salt Lake City and nursing school, my stepmother announced a change in plans.

"I've had a letter from your father," she said. "We can't afford to send you to Holy Cross. You're going to have to go to a local college."

I was crushed. All my plans had to be discarded. Salt Lake City was to have been the beginning of my new life. Why did I have to change my plans? But I swallowed my feelings and accepted her word as final.

It hurt as I wrote the nursing school to say I wasn't coming. Reluctantly, I wrote to Tempe and was accepted there.

Many years later—when I was thirty-two, in fact—I learned that my father had never written that letter. It was my *stepmother* who had written *to him* to say, "Pat has changed her mind. She doesn't want to go to Holy Cross. She wants to go to Arizona State in Tempe instead. And that will be good, because it's less expensive."

At Tempe I met Allen again. He was a sophomore. I was just "one of the girls from Jerome." To my surprise, Allen found my residence on campus and before long we were dating. I began to feel that Allen was the most wonderful thing that had ever happened to me. We were very much in love.

We planned a June wedding and a honeymoon in Mexico. I was counting the days and dreaming.

But once more my stepmother changed our plans. "My military travel orders have come through," she reported. "I must leave in May to join your father in Japan."

Her plans made no difference to me. I had no intention of changing the date and sacrificing our honeymoon. We'd get married without her.

But Allen's parents felt differently. "At least one of your parents should be at the wedding," they said. I couldn't tell them how I felt about my stepmother. They wouldn't understand. Reluctantly, I agreed to change the date.

Allen and I were married on April 3, during the four-day Easter break. We didn't have a honeymoon trip. There wasn't time.

And my stepmother? She left for Japan in August, just as she had planned originally. Meanwhile, she wrote my father, explaining that we had moved our wedding date up because I was pregnant and couldn't wait until June.

My father wrote me a scathing letter, telling me what my stepmother had reported and how disappointed he was in me. "I didn't think my daughter would ever do anything like that!" he wrote in anger.

I wasn't surprised at what my stepmother had done. She had done that kind of thing all her life. But I had always held on to the hope that my father hadn't believed her stories. I had hoped he could see through what she was doing. But without even asking me what had happened, he had believed her whole story. I was crushed. How could he believe that woman?

When Allen saw the letter he was very supportive. At least here was *someone* who loved me. And his father's response was, "I will be your father. If this is all he thinks of you, all he trusts you, you don't need him as a father." In the midst of my pain and the feelings of rejection, I was being loved and supported. And that felt *so* good.

Allen was going to be responsible for me. That made me willing to change my personal goals. Now it became important for me to help him through school. I really felt privileged to help him achieve his goal, rather than to marry him after he had accomplished it. This way I could feel like a contributor, a part of the effort, someone deserving of the benefits we would earn together in the future.

That feeling came from my father's influence. Over the years he had built into me the need to feel deserving of the things I received. And just as deeply, he had planted the feeling that I didn't deserve much. No matter what I did, I was always short of the mark.

If I brought home good grades from school, that's what I was "supposed" to do. "You want me to tell you this is wonderful? This isn't wonderful. It's what my daughter is *supposed* to do." When I won an award, "My daughter is supposed to win awards." If I got a promotion, "My daughter is supposed to get to the top."

I cannot remember one single time that my father made me feel approved. Whatever I did, it was only what he expected. After all, I was *his* daughter.

With that kind of upbringing, the need to give up my personal goals and help Allen accomplish his was only logical. If there was to be a bright future for me, I would have to "earn" it.

After only four months of marriage, in Allen's junior year in college, I had emergency surgery. Eight feet of my small intestine were removed. In spite of our insurance, the surgery ate up every penny Allen had saved.

Because our money was gone, Allen decided he would join the Marines for two years. When he came out, he reasoned, he could finish his schooling under the GI Bill.

We had spent all of *Allen's* money on *my* surgery. Now, because of me, he was changing his educational plans. I felt guilty. This was all my fault. *You just can't do anything right, Pat,* I said to myself.

It wasn't anything Allen did or said. Really, he took the changes in stride. The feelings of failure were something I did to myself. I wasn't holding up "my end of the bargain." And look at what was happening. Look at the mess we were in.

After boot camp, Allen was stationed in San Francisco. We were together again, and things were progressing well. After three years of marriage, our first daughter, Jennifer, was born. That was an exciting time. I had *really* wanted to have a baby. And this beautiful little girl was everything we could have hoped for.

After Allen's discharge, he enrolled in a pre-veterinary medicine program at UC Davis. We were on our way back to school. It was the beginning of a long, hard, emotionally wrenching time for both of us. I wanted very much to stay at home and raise our daughter. But we couldn't afford that. Instead, I went to work full time. And the tension between what I *needed* to do and what I *wanted* to do ate at my insides.

A part of me knew how difficult it was to get grades good enough to be accepted into veterinary school. And I knew how important that schooling was for Allen . . . and for me. But another part of me saw other husbands working and getting good grades and getting into veterinary school. *Their* wives stayed at home and cared for the children. Why couldn't *I?* The question wouldn't go away.

There was no escaping the fact that we were beginning to grow farther and farther apart. I wanted something out of life *now.* But for Allen, everything was seen in terms of goal-setting. The future would be rosy if we only kept our noses to the grindstone now.

"When I get into vet school, everything is going to be all right."

Later on, when he was in vet school, it was, "When I graduate, everything will be all right then."

Then it was, "When I get my doctor's degree, then we'll start making it."

And when he got the degree, it became, "When I get my own clinic. . ." We were always looking to the future. There was going to be pie in some far-off sky in some by-and-by that seemed like it would never come.

I was always saying, "What about today? What about our needs right now?"

Allen's answer was always, "You don't understand. We've got to build for the future."

With the chasm between us widening, I began to feel that Allen didn't really love me. He never seemed to hear what I was saying, or, if he heard, he didn't seem to care anymore. I felt he was just using me to help him reach his goal.

As a result, my feelings began to do flip-flops. Sometimes I would be down in the dumps. My world had turned dark. Other times I would pick myself up and decide to be happy. I put on a happy face, but I knew it wasn't real.

My constant changes were too much for him. "Pat," he would complain, "I don't know what I'm going to find when I get home. I don't know if I'm going to have a wife who is down in the dumps or up in the clouds. I'd sure like to see a little stability around here."

In the midst of this, our second daughter, Karen, was born. It was during Allen's final exams. He took me to the hospital the night she was born, and he came back to the hospital seven days later to bring us home. Not *once* did he come to visit us.

I knew he was studying for finals, but I couldn't help feeling unloved and uncared for. At least he would want to see Karen, wouldn't he?

He did call me daily. It was, "Hello, how are you? How's

the baby?" Then, having satisfied himself as to the state of our health, he would launch into a gloomy report of how poorly he was doing in his tests.

My feelings of being a convenience for Allen grew deeper. More and more I felt as if I was the woman who was to work *and* pay the bills *and* fix the dinner *and* take care of the kids *and* sweep the floors *and* put Allen through school. If I wasn't there he would get along. But I sure was a convenience.

When he brought us home from the hospital, he had "a suggestion." Jennifer was visiting her grandparents. "When I'm studying for finals, I need my rest," he reminded me. "I'm staying up late and studying. You're breast-feeding the baby, so I can't help you feed her. Instead of waking both of us, why doesn't she just wake you? So why don't you sleep in Jennifer's room?"

Everything was very logical. There was no way a reasonable person could argue against his "suggestion." But I was devastated. I was being put out of my own bedroom, no longer wanted by my husband until, of course, my presence would no longer be an inconvenience. Yet I dutifully agreed, and followed his "suggestion."

That day something snapped inside of me. I should have been excited that something new was beginning. After all, here was a beautiful new baby who was going to enrich our lives. Instead, lying in a lonely bed that night with only Karen beside me, I felt as if something had ended. Yet, I couldn't cry. There were no tears. I felt overwhelmed by a cold, heavy sense of loss. My marriage had died. It might be years before it was buried, but that day, that painful day . . . it died.

* * *

Driving down the road I suddenly noticed a freeway sign that said San Jose. I was close to my destination. The familiarity of the surroundings brought a flood of memories to melt my coldness. I was beginning to feel again, but my feelings were those of bitterness and resentment against Allen, mixed with a strong case of anger at myself. "This was the right thing to do," I assured myself. "Get out of his life. You can get along better without him. He hasn't provided us with the things he should, things like a home or an income. *You've* provided that. He hasn't loved you. Just look at all the painful memories you've been facing this afternoon. Get out. Leave him. You can take care of yourself."

I was trying to put steel into my resolve. As I slowly lost a grip on my life, I was frantically reaching down somewhere inside for support. And it worked. *I convinced myself I had been done in.*

It was late afternoon as I pulled up in front of my uncle's and aunt's home. They came out to greet me, and as soon as I saw them the floodgates burst, and I began to sob. I cried. And I cried. And I cried.

They held me close, and with my tears all the bravado I had begun to build up was washed away. The memory of all the painful things Allen had done to me slowly faded. What had been a vivid recollection only a short time ago now seemed distant to me.

Where the pain had been I now began to feel a terrible sense of loss. I groaned inside, rocked by the realization that the marriage was over. And there was absolutely nothing I could do to put it back together again. Nothing. Now I could see more clearly that I was as big a contributor to the failure of the marriage as Allen had been. We shared the responsibility. No; maybe it was even more my fault than his. I didn't want it to end, but now I had gone too far.

Now it was over. Such awful finality. I still loved Allen. I loved Jennifer and Karen. I didn't want to lose my family and my home. But there was nothing, *nothing I could do.*

CHAPTER 4

Divided, I Fall

I stayed with my uncle and aunt for a week. Time and time again during the early part of the week I gave way to tears of hopelessness. Then, at midweek, I called my father in San Bernardino, California. Both he and my uncle felt there was still hope for the marriage. They convinced me not to file for the divorce right away.

"Take a few days to think things over," they suggested. "Then go back to Allen and ask him to give you another chance."

The more I thought about it, the more I could see their wisdom. Perhaps we could straighten things out if we got some professional help. Maybe our marriage would even be stronger because of the problems we had faced together. It was worth a try. My tears began to give way to joyful planning.

I was going back to Allen. We would seek help together. We would make this thing work. After all, this would be best for everyone, wouldn't it?

There was no room in my plans for Allen to say no. The lives of our daughters and our years of work and sacrifice were at stake. How could he possibly deny us one more opportunity to save our marriage? Surely he wouldn't say no. He couldn't.

I wrapped myself in a romantic dream straight out of a 1936 movie, swallowed my pride, and arranged to meet Allen in the parking lot of the Edgewater Inn in Oakland. That was his suggestion—"It would be best if we're on neutral ground."

My cousins drove up with me from San Jose. All during the trip I rehearsed what I would say. There was no use in trying, "You've hurt me. You've done this. You've done that." *I* would take all the blame. There wasn't any other way. "I'm guilty. I'm sorry. Please forgive me. Can we find something to build on?"

We met in the parking lot. I said my piece, and I meant every word of it. "I'll go to anybody," I pleaded. "I'll go to a preacher, a psychiatrist, a psychologist. Anybody. You tell me who. You're the boss. We'll go together or I'll go alone, whatever you say."

"Yes, Pat, you need help," I remember him saying. "But *I* don't. You are too emotional. Your highs are too high. Your lows are too low. I just can't take it any longer. I want out."

The conversation seemed to go nowhere. Or did he have a script he'd memorized?

"You can get some counseling if you want to. In fact, you probably should. But I'm not going to be involved. Our marriage is over. NO."

He turned and walked back to his car.

I was stunned. Everything in me seemed to ache as I watched him drive away.

I had pinned all my hopes on this meeting. We *had* to get back together. Allen *had* to forgive me. We *had* to try again. There was no other way.

Now all of that was ended. The light had gone out on my movie-like dream of reunion, and I was left alone. All around me in the parking lot people were coming and going. It was a busy place. But in the midst of it all, my world had stopped dead still.

I felt the bitter pain of rejection, the pain of having come back repentant, pleading, heart in hand—only to be turned away.

Then slowly a new emotion took over. I felt an urge to run away, to get out of there, as if something inside me sought to reinforce my new "aloneness." That was it. I had to escape. I set an emotional crash course for Las Vegas—and a divorce.

Hastily I found my cousins in the hotel coffee shop. I can't even remember explaining what had happened. How do you tell a bystander that out there in the parking lot you tried to put your marriage back together and failed?

An hour down the freeway, in San Jose, I dropped my cousins at their home and hurriedly got back on the road. There was no time to pack a bag. The few things I had in the car would be enough. After all, what kind of things did one pack for a divorce?

Each mile toward Nevada brought more ache and a deeper sense of loss. With the ache came the hope that the day would come when I would no longer have to feel deep emotion. Perhaps I could lock my heart away in a steel box. Nobody could reach it there. Nothing could disturb it. And I could go on living, without feelings.

But as good as that idea sounded, I couldn't think of any way to bring it about. It seemed I was doomed to go on feeling. And hurting. And feeling some more. And hurting some more.

No, there *was* a way. I'd been treated like an old shoe—worn for a while and then thrown away. I wasn't considered worth repairing. I had been used. Now it was time to be the user. But how? Then my answer came. I would become a hard old boot. I would be impenetrable; water, snow, ice . . . pain, heartache, even love—none of those things would get to me. I would face the elements, wipe myself off, and survive. Never again would anyone throw *me* away. No one would *dare*. I would be too strong.

Pain and resolve were mixed in monumental proportions on that lonely trip to Las Vegas. But the closer I got to Nevada and its famous quickie divorce, the more the pain seemed to give way to a cold resolve. Never, never, never, I told myself, would I be used again.

When I arrived in the gaudy capital of show and sham, my resolve quickly began to disappear. It seemed I wasn't made of such hardy stuff after all. I felt overwhelmed and frightened. I was here to get a divorce, but nobody was here to give me a handy do-it-yourself guide to Nevada divorce. I was on my own, and I was scared.

I found a motel. It hurt as I signed "Mrs. Allen. . ." and then changed it to "Mrs. Pat. . . ." The second step was to go to bed. There would be time enough tomorrow to start this whole ugly divorce business.

The next day I looked for a lawyer in the yellow pages of the phone book. In a strange town, from a strange list of names, how do you select the man who will help you dissolve twelve years of marriage?

I chose one with the same last name as the obstetrician who had delivered our younger daughter. That obstetrician had been supportive and caring, and maybe I hoped those qualities went with the name. I suppose a familiar name gave me some sense of security in this frightening new world.

The lawyer did give me a very definite sense of security. He had been through this many times before, and yet for all his professionalism he seemed to care about what was happening. I liked him. Even having a practiced professional "care" about me felt good at that painful point in my life.

He told me that the rules were few and simple. *I could not leave the state for forty-four days!* When we went to court, I must have a witness who could testify to having seen me at least once in every twenty-four-hour period during those days.

He suggested that I ask the desk clerk at the motel to be my witness. The desk clerk—a witness at my divorce? That idea embarrassed me, but it seemed like an easy solution.

Back at my motel I went to the lobby. Trying to look nonchalant, I studied the magazines. Finally I gathered up my courage and approached the desk clerk. I barely got out the words, "My lawyer said . . ." when she nodded her understanding.

"Oh, yeah," she said. "That costs ten dollars. You can give me the money the day you go to court."

Then, without another question from me, she explained the whole process. She must see me every day. A telephone call wouldn't do. On my day in court, she would be there to testify.

The process was almost painless. But there was still the nagging sense of hopelessness inside of me. I had been sentenced to singleness, forced to break up my family. And I responded by spending the next forty-four days sleeping. It was my escape. When you are sleeping you don't have to think. You don't have to feel. Time seems to pass quickly.

My days slipped into an almost mechanical routine. At three each afternoon I would get up, take a shower, and get dressed. On my way to the restaurant next door to the motel, I would greet the desk clerk or wave at her through the window. Then, as part of the routine, I would have a hamburger and a milkshake and buy a paperback book—usually a detective story.

During my waking hours I buried myself in Agatha Christie. Back in my motel room I could sometimes read halfway through the book before falling asleep. Most nights I would awaken in the middle of the night, finish the book, then go back to sleep until it was time to start the listless, lifeless experience all over again.

Through all the machine-like process of those days, I sensed that this was a period of incubation for me. The new person I was going to be was being fashioned in those forty-four days in a cheap Las Vegas motel. Yet this realization brought a new frustration.

What was I becoming? On one hand I was determined not to feel. I would learn to use people rather than be used by them. I wanted desperately to be a strong, impenetrable fortress.

But I faced another almost opposite concern. With everything in me I did not want to become a bitter, resentful woman. I would not allow myself to be vindictive. A nagging suspicion said that Allen had been *right* to ask for this divorce. He knew how impossible I had been to live with. He was much more of a realist than I, and I should be gratified that he had the sense to call a halt to this fruitless marriage.

To this confusing mixture of feelings I added still

another thought. "This is the end of your marriage," I reminded myself. "It is not the end of your life, Pat. The cooking, the housekeeping, the endless ironing—that's over. You're free now. You'll soon have no husband to please or cater to, no one to give you false hopes and dreams. Life isn't too bad after all. You're free. Free. Free."

Each of these feelings was very much a part of me. Each begged for recognition. But rather than deal with any one feeling in depth or make any kind of sense of the feelings, I chose my sleep-and-Agatha-Christie remedy. And it worked.

The forty-fourth day finally arrived. This was my day in court. I met my attorney in his office, and we walked together to the courtroom. My ten-dollar witness was there, just as she had promised.

I remember that the judge looked very much like a judge I had once seen in a movie. I remember my name being called. I walked forward and sat in the witness stand. There were questions, and I must have answered them. But all of that is a blur, a painful experience, a life-changing moment lost in the protective shadows of a faded memory.

I remember stepping down and walking out of the courtroom into the hallway.

My attorney followed, smiling. "You did just fine," he reassured me. Then his voice seemed to change. "Well, it's all over. May I buy you a drink? It's a tradition here in Nevada, you know. The attorney always buys the divorcée a drink after her day in court. Then we'll go throw your wedding ring away if you want to. There are lots of fountains around here that have seen more than one wedding band.

"Come on, Pat," his voice bounced on. "It's time to celebrate. You're free now."

I was stunned. My twelve years of married life were over. *Ended.* It was as if I had gone to sleep only a few days ago and had awakened *divorced.* I had lost forever something that had been a vital part of me. And now I was to have a drink with my lawyer and throw my wedding ring in a fountain?

Deep inside, like an echo in an underground cave, rang the thought: *My marriage is over.*

Five minutes. It had only taken five minutes to wipe out twelve whole years. The good times and the bad were all gone.

I turned to my lawyer and heard myself say, "Sure. Why not?"

Sinking, I grabbed at a straw of hope. That dark inner echo became the bright voice of a new day. "This isn't the end, Pat," it seemed to say. "This is the beginning."

And it was.

As most divorced persons do, I began to sense this exhilarating new freedom, like a brisk wind in your sails. In your better moments you dream of the open seas, the vast new life ahead of you. You reach for the rudder.

And, in panic, you find it isn't there.

All the old rules that guided you, the familiar places, the faces, the old routines—life's little rituals— everything is gone. No, not gone. Very little is changed. The old faces, the old places are still there. *You're* the one who has changed. And that first breath of freedom—that glimpse of the open seas—that new life ahead soon becomes a frontier struggle for survival.

Looking back, I don't really remember making any hard choices. At least not the "what-will-I-do-with-the-rest-of-my-life" kind of choices. My choices were simply *survival* choices.

We finished our drinks. Now, one of my first decisions was to get outside the four walls of that little motel room. The intense loneliness I felt there was more than I could handle. Somehow the gaudy plastic, the empty plastic of that room seemed hour after endless hour to mock the stark emptiness and loneliness of my life.

I had to find people somewhere. I had to see faces—any faces.

And I found them in a local bar. There you could step in easily and become one of the group. No questions were ever asked.

Returning night after night, I began to have a sense of belonging to something. The chatter was always light, always superficial. Best of all, the bar scene kept me from having to think and feel about what was going on in my life.

There was something else I remembered about that bar. It offered a graduate program in emptiness. Like all the rest of the "students," my major was false facade development. People had names, but those names were not their real names. Many times the jobs they talked about weren't their real jobs.

Everyone's hurts were too deep or, perhaps, too recent to permit the luxury of reality. We lived in the world of the lie; we created a world we wished was ours.

I lied if it served some purpose. I lied about what I was doing or where I was going or how old I was or anything I felt like lying about. If I thought it would protect me, I lied. Somehow it was the natural thing to do.

All the bar regulars became my friends, but I never saw them outside the bar. We didn't do the normal "friend" things. We never went to each other's homes. That would be too revealing. Strangely, I can't remember the name of even one of those "friends."

Yet, for all their emptiness—and mine, too—they reached out to touch me at a time of desperate need. I know their touch was often phony. It was given too casually to be real. I knew I was as phony as anyone else, and I didn't like it. But I belonged there. These were people who had been where I was, and that gave us a strange sense of fellowship, of belonging.

When I had first arrived in Las Vegas to file for divorce, I was totally dependent on Allen. Every penny I had came from him. The motel bill, the food—he paid for everything. I would call and talk to the girls. Then it was, "Let me talk to Dad."

"Allen, I have to pay the rent next week and I need some more money."

"Well, I sent you a hundred dollars. What did you do with that?"

I would report as best I could how the money was spent. After his regular disclaimer ("I just don't have it to send to you, Pat"), he would agree to send what he could. And he did.

But that was *so* painful. I felt like a beggar. And out of that discomfort came my second survival decision: get a job.

I had planned to return to San Francisco, but mere survival dictated otherwise. I took what experience I had, added a few lies to make my work background sound better than it really was, and got a job working for Clark County, Nevada, as a computer programmer. I found an apartment in Las Vegas. My job was in the courthouse.

No one in Las Vegas seemed to care much about *who*

you were or what your marital status was. It made no difference. Millions of people came here each year to forget who they were, even if just for a few days. One more unknown casualty was easily swallowed up in the tawdry tinsel of this desert city.

My only ties to reality and warmth were my frequent phone conversations with Jennifer and Karen. Those precious minutes were full of the questions one asks eight- and nine-year-old girls.

"How are you?"

"What are you doing?"

"What's happening at school?"

"What do you want for your birthday?"

And they were full of pain.

"Mom, we're having a play. Can you come?"

Behind my "No, dear, I can't" was a deep sense of guilt because I wasn't with them. Had I been a better mother, I would be there, I felt.

And, in what I felt were my more honest moments, I knew they were better off with Allen than with me. After all, he was the "good guy" and I was the "bad guy."

Being away from the girls was sometimes more than I could handle, so I would fly to San Francisco to see them. No sooner would I arrive than I would discover that I didn't like being with them. Oh, make no mistake, we filled every moment with love. I paid attention to every word of the eight- and nine-year-old small talk I had so easily disregarded before. But I knew that in just a few short hours I would be leaving them. There was so much I wanted to do with them and say to them. I wanted to be with them; my arms ached to hold them and never let go. And my heart was sad. In my brightest "hello" there now had to be a painful "good-bye."

But I had no one to share that pain with—not even the people at the bar.

So I told myself I didn't really care. I put on a smile, and if anyone asked, everything was going "great . . . just *great*, thank you." Everyone I knew handled hurts by acting like they didn't exist or weren't important anyway. I was learning to play that game.

Then something began to break into that empty life-style, that life-style of the lie. It started when an old friend of my father introduced me to a man.

"He's a lawyer," my father's old school mate told me. "Very progressive. A real comer. Someday he's going to be the governor of Nevada."

I went out with him a few times. Our dates were always during the daytime. At first I couldn't figure out why. "Las Vegas is an upside down kind of town," I said to myself, "but dates are still a nighttime thing."

Then on a Saturday evening date with another fellow, I saw my "up-and-coming lawyer." He was the head waiter in the restaurant where we were having dinner.

I was entangled in the web of the constant lie. And I had the first vague feelings of wanting to get out of all this, of wanting something better. But I did nothing about it. Everybody lived by the lie. Why should I be different?

Dating another man brought me to my senses. We had gone out a number of times over a period of weeks.

Then one day I got an angry phone call. "Leave my husband alone," the unnamed voice said. She hung up. I hadn't known he was married. My boss had introduced us and he hadn't mentioned a wife and a family.

I put down the phone and headed straight for my boss's office. Without knocking I barged in.

"That guy's married," I reported.

He looked up, and with a strange look on his face he said, "Sure. Didn't you know?"

"I've got to get out of this place," I said out loud. "It's all a pack of lies."

"Of course it is," my boss responded. "Nobody in Las Vegas wants you to know where they have come from or where they're going, who they are or what they are doing. They're here for only one reason, and that is simply to escape probing personal questions."

I had no idea what I would do or where I would go. But I quit on the spot.

CHAPTER 5

The Second Time Around

San Francisco. City by the bay. I love you, San Francisco. The weather is perfect. What a place to begin *another* new life and to wash away the stains of Las Vegas.

The decision to return wasn't a conscious decision. There really wasn't anything else for me to do. San Francisco was a familiar place, and I needed a familiar place. Jennifer and Karen were there. That's all that was left of home.

And I had one more tie: old friends from my married days—the rare kind that remained friends *after* the divorce. Paul and Theresa had often said, "When you're ready to come home, you've got a home here. You can stay with us until you get a job."

I did. And before long I got a job. It was just what my sagging self-image needed.

My Las Vegas graduate course in lying helped. I let Macy's of California "assume" that I had worked on their kind of computer longer than I had. It worked. I was hired as the number two person in their new data processing department. That made me a junior executive, an important status position.

"You've been down, Pat, and you're on your way up," I told myself. "Forge ahead, whatever the cost."

Part of the cost was to bury myself in my work. That was sure to pay big dividends. It was a way to move up a few more rungs on the prestige ladder. And I would have another success story to add to Pat's all-too-slim book of accomplishments.

Those were the early days of data processing. Programmers and computer systems engineers were special people, members of a kind of fraternity. I did whatever was necessary to make myself a part of that fraternity. This elite group became *mine.* They were my sophisticated replacement for the Las Vegas bar.

Whereas in Vegas, I went to a bar to *find* a group, here I went to the bar *with* a group. We could have gone to an ice-cream parlor instead of a bar. Where we were going wasn't important. Belonging was the important thing.

These relationships were different from those in Las Vegas, I assured myself. They felt different. But they weren't, really.

My apartment was not just *any* apartment. Mine was a *front* apartment—on the top floor, on a hill, with a fireplace, a view—and, above all, a good address. Most of my friends had first-floor apartments, in the back, with no fireplace and no view.

My apartment was charming, but even now I can remember not really feeling at home there. There was a temporary feeling about the place. I felt I was just "staying" there. I moved in with a sense of excitement about all the things I was going to do to make it homey, but I never did a single one of them.

I know now that my temporary feeling had nothing to do with the apartment. But it had everything to do with how I felt about myself. It took me many years and many apartments before I ever felt at home.

I bought a new car—a GTO.

I bought new clothes at all the right stores.

I had *things*.

But I kept relationships on a strictly professional and superficial level. It was safer that way. If you keep busy, there is no time to think about loneliness. Who's lonely? Not me. See how busy I am?

I never ate breakfast. Since early childhood, breakfast had been a formal family meal, a big meal with everybody at the table. Allen and I had continued that custom. Now breakfast held too many painful memories, memories I could forget if I just didn't eat.

Eating at home *at all* meant the stirring up of memories. It always seemed empty at the table, and that was more than I could handle. So I ate out far more than I needed to (or could afford to). Whenever possible, I ate *with* someone. Anyone. My rare meal at home was always eaten in the living room from a TV tray. There were fewer memories that way.

And what an escape sleep was. When there was nothing else to do—no group to meet with, no project to complete— I could sleep, sleep, sleep and escape, escape, escape.

For all the security I found in my group, I was slowly learning to count on only one person: Pat. I didn't need anybody. I was self-sufficient. Things were working for me. I was doing it all by *myself*. *For* myself.

Most of the time I remember feeling that life was good—maybe not *great*, but good. I didn't hurt any more. I didn't *let* myself hurt. But in my mad dash to keep from hurting, something else happened—something I had not expected. I lost the ability to feel any emotion.

On the street I could see a beggar and feel no sympathy at all. After all, he could get out of that life if he wanted to. I had. I'd been a beggar, and I'd gotten up on my own two feet and started a new life with precious little help from anyone. And if I can do it, beggar, *so can you.* You'll get no help from me.

I was beginning to feel like the statues in Golden Gate Park. Cold. Unfeeling. But that was a good way to be, or at least it was safe. And it meant that I was in control, right where I wanted to be. "Who needs to feel, anyway? Not me," I assured myself.

Right into the midst of my careful "control" came the first stable relationship in my new single life. It came about because of my job.

I spent a three-day weekend with the girl who was my IBM systems engineer. Together we were designing a new system for our computer. She let *me* design the system. She answered questions and made coffee and sandwiches, but she let me do the work.

In the process I found that I liked her. I trusted her, and she trusted me.

It all began at a very professional level. We were doing a job together. But sometime during the weekend my "control" began to slip. Something reached me at a personal level. I felt the beginnings of a friendship. But I was determined to keep that friendship at a purely professional level. That's where I kept everything: strictly professional.

Just like my group at the Vegas bar, my IBM group was important to me. They were my security base. With them

I was never alone in public. I didn't have to worry about being attractive or trying to make friends. I always had my group. If, on occasion, I reached out to someone on a one-to-one basis, the risks were minimized because I had my group. If I was turned down or turned off, I could always run back to my group instead of going home to lick my wounds.

I performed to be accepted, just to belong. And I kept on performing for their approval by working hard and well. I performed by being very loyal to IBM equipment and by learning how to make it work more efficiently. I performed for my boss at Macy's and my financial vice-president.

Everything I did was calculated to enhance my performance. Every morning I spread the stage curtains, and at night I slowly closed them in the privacy of my own apartment. Or maybe I never really closed them. Perhaps they were open all the time. Perhaps I was always on stage, and even performed for myself.

I was a very lonely, empty person, but I never admitted that even to myself. The performance went on, and I found it easy to perform. I even told *myself* that everything was "just fine, thank you."

Men singled me out in a group, and that was flattering. I loved the attention, but if I dated a man it was because he had passed my three basic tests: He was attractive; he made good money; and he was doing something interesting with his life.

When the talk in my group got around to the men I was dating, I talked about "the doctor," "the lawyer," or the "vice-president." It was never "this really neat fellow. . . ."

Men were trophies to be collected. The last thing I

wanted was to be emotionally involved with any man. Men were a convenience, and as soon as they became an inconvenience, I dropped them.

I could maintain a relationship with a man for several weeks, even for several months. But it was never an exclusive arrangement. I would gladly cancel one date for what I considered to be a better opportunity with a "better" man.

After all, if you're out for status, the right place for a date is important. If I had one dinner invitation to a very nice place and another to an even nicer place—a really "in" place—I chose the "in" place. Being seen there, or reporting that I'd been there, made me feel important and valuable, and I fed on that.

Then Dick entered the picture. One of the really nice guys of this world, he was an executive with a major corporation, and he was recently divorced. In the beginning, everything was simple. We just dated. We had dinner during the week or an occasional weekend date.

Then, slowly, things began to change. He told me he loved me. I really liked Dick. He was a good and gentle man. But *love* him? Not me. Remember, this is the woman with no emotional entanglements. It's all just for the fun, Dick, okay?

He kept saying, "I love you, Pat," and waiting for me to say, "I love you, too, Dick." But I couldn't say that. I *wouldn't* say that. Even if I had thought I loved him I wouldn't have said it.

The problem wasn't simply saying the words. It was what I knew would come after the words. For after "I love you" would come "I want to marry you and live with you." I couldn't do that. I didn't want to do that.

The moment he asked for that kind of involvement was

the end. He wanted an emotional investment from me, one I could not or would not give. And so Dick quietly walked out of my life.

Somehow I walked away from the short-lived relationship completely unscathed. He may have suffered in the break, but I don't even remember thinking about that. He had once been a part of my life; now he was gone.

In a rare moment of honesty, however, I felt myself being sucked down into an ugly, dark cave. Each cold, calculating move on my part was pulling me farther down. I had *not* walked away from Dick unscathed. Instead, I had sunk a little deeper, and I knew it.

"It can't be true," I argued with myself. "I have it *all* now. I'm right where I should be, right where I planned to be."

But, more and more, I knew that was a lie. One day, one dark day, I caught a glimpse of the rotten me. The image was so real I could almost smell the stench. I remember walking into the bathroom and looking at myself in the mirror. The Pat I saw was old. And hard.

I gritted my teeth, clenched my fists, and with every bit of energy I could muster I screamed at that dark figure in the looking glass.

"GO TO HELL! Somebody . . . anybody, get that horrible woman out of my life." Then, in a moment, from deep inside me came, "I DON'T CARE. I'll be who I am."

I steeled myself and turned away from that fleeting moment of honesty. I wasn't going to soften or give in.

My relationship to Paul and Theresa was the one small crack in my hardness. They were the one reminder that inside of me—deep inside—was a person who longed to be loved, to belong, to be at home in a relationship, to reach out and care. The warmth of their relationship and the warmth they shared with me was the one thing that managed to melt my hardness . . . just a little.

Paul and Theresa hadn't had a night on the town in months. There was no money for luxuries. Theresa had leukemia, and her treatment was taking every cent they had. But for one night Pat was going to change that. They were going to celebrate. No, *we* were going to celebrate together.

"I am going to give you a hundred dollars, and the three of us are going to go out and have a good time. You've done all kinds of things for me. Now I want to do something special for you." And celebrate we did. It was a good evening. Good friends. Good food. Good wine. The restaurant owner was a friend of Paul's, and he gave us his personal attention.

Throughout dinner, I felt the special warmth that comes from giving, and it made me feel like a living, breathing person again. The hardness would be back in the morning, but for tonight it was gone. As we sipped after-dinner drinks and laughed over shared memories, the owner stopped at our table to introduce a friend.

We met Jim—broad shouldered, muscular, and pleasant. We invited him to join us, and he took the chair next to me. As we got acquainted, we found that Jim was a mechanical engineer. He'd done some very interesting work and had been on assignments in Alaska and South America. I was impressed, and I liked him.

I liked him enough that, when he called me a day later, I agreed to go out with him. Later on, I found he would not have taken no for an answer. It seems that the first night in the restaurant, before he was introduced and joined our threesome, he had decided that he was in love with me. As far as Jim was concerned, it was a foregone conclusion that we would be married. It was just a matter of time.

"But hold on, Jim. I'm dating other guys. I'm not serious about you," I would protest.

And his response was always the same. "You will be. That's how you feel right now, but you'll change."

He was serious. I wasn't. He was adoring. I loved his adoration, but I didn't love *him.* All the attention he lavished on me was very flattering. I was getting the love I had always hoped for. I was special to someone—very special. And since he required almost nothing in return, I soaked up all the affection he was willing to give.

There was one concern . . . one little cloud on this loving horizon. Jim drank too much. But I put it out of my mind. I wasn't serious about him, so why worry?

He gave me things. Boy, did he give me things. Anything I wanted. Nothing was too good for me. He took me anyplace I wanted to go. If I wanted to go skiing, Jim took me skiing. He didn't ski, but he took me and sat in the lodge, drinking and waiting for me to come down off the hill.

He took me horseback riding. He didn't ride, but he took me to the stables and waited three or four hours until I had ridden as long as I wanted. I wanted to learn to fly. Jim wasn't interested in flying. But without any complaint, he drove me out to my lesson and, when it was over, he brought me back.

It was like a fairy tale. My wish was his command. I could have anything I wanted. We dated for seven months, and those months of adoration broke my resistance to Jim's constant talk of marriage.

I didn't love Jim. That had not changed. And I told him so again and again. One night, it seemed as if the time for straight talk had arrived. If this relationship was going anywhere at all, it was going there on *my* terms. It was time to be brutally honest.

"The only people I love are Jennifer and Karen," I started out. "I don't love you. You know that. I don't even *want* to love you. I like you and maybe even admire you. You drink a little too much, but if that's your only fault I can tolerate that as long as it doesn't happen too frequently, and you don't embarrass me in front of my friends."

There was more. I was merciless. There would be no question about whether or not he had heard my terms loud and clear.

"If you ever try to come between me and my daughters, you will lose. They are my number-one priority.

"That's the way things are and they aren't likely to change. If you are willing to accept that, I'll marry you."

It sounded like an ultimatum, because it *was* an ultimatum. It wasn't exactly the most timid response to a marriage proposal. But it was honest. I had said yes—the word I had vowed *never* to say again. Why I was saying it now, I couldn't understand.

Before Jim could answer, I thought of one more ultimatum. "My money is *my* money. I'll continue to work. After all, my career is important to me. And besides, I won't be left at the mercy of any man. I'll contribute to our living expenses, but my money will be mine. What you do with your money is your responsibility, as long as you don't ever expect me to support you."

From deep inside I heaved a sigh. My feelings were

mixed. I had just agreed to marriage. But it hurt. There were no soft feelings of love; instead, I felt as if I had won the upper hand in a painful process of negotiation.

Could this be a marriage? Whatever gentle part of me still lived cried an almost unheard "No!" But another part of me felt very safe. I was playing it smart. This man adored me, but he could never hurt me because I wouldn't let him. It *was* a negotiation, and I did have the upper hand. No romantic notions would trick me into surrendering that hand. I remember looking in the mirror and renewing my vow to win, no matter what the cost. I felt hollow. Something in me was dying that night. But I did nothing to stop the process. I couldn't, or maybe I *wouldn't.*

Jim responded as he had many times before. "Pat, I love you enough for both of us. Someday you will come to love me, too."

"Don't count on it," I said, not wanting to leave any doubt about where I stood.

The next Saturday we drove to Reno to be married. The weather was fantastic—clear, crisp, and sunny. We drove through some of the most magnificent country in all the West. We saw majestic mountains, crystal clear lakes, and rugged Donner Pass. I had driven this road before and been captivated by its beauty.

But this time the warmth, the beauty, and the celebration were a million miles away.

Despite the sunshine, I was cold with an emotional chill that made me shiver. I looked across the car at the man I was about to marry and knew more clearly than ever that I was making a mistake. Doggedly, deliberately, *I was doing the wrong thing.*

Trying to shake my feelings, I reminded myself of our

agreement. This man adored me, yet didn't expect anything from me. He knew how I felt. I had been transparently honest with him, and he still loved me, just as I was and just as I would always be. I shouldn't be expected to feel loving now, or ever. That wasn't part of our bargain.

I had played my cards right this time. I had learned to hold out for the things that were the most important to me. My daughters came first. I'd made that clear. They were getting along just fine. Their father was supporting them, leaving me free of that financial worry. It was a joy to watch them develop and to buy things for them.

I had forged a career for myself in data processing that was the envy of most women I knew. And now the crowning accomplishment: I had an adoring man who asked almost nothing of me in return.

Of course, everything would be fine. Everything was fine *already*. All the important things I could ever want were at my fingertips.

Be quiet, heart. Listen to the calculating voice of reason.

So it was that I reasoned my way into a second marriage, into the little wedding chapel and through the brief, almost mechanical ceremony.

Then I got absolutely dead drunk. The more I drank, the happier I got. I sang. I danced. I loved everybody. Everything was wonderful. With each drink, my wedding felt less and less like the funeral it really had been. Lift your glass, Pat, and have another. Here's to the wedding. The next morning I had a terrible hangover and a monstrous headache.

And . . . a husband.

As we drove back to Jim's home in Oakland, there were no little-girl-like hopes for married bliss. The little girl had died long ago, and in her place was a cold, calculating woman. This woman had made a pretty good deal, and she was going to live up to her end of this business venture, and nothing more.

Now let's get home to Oakland and get on with the adoration, I thought. That's why I got into this crazy relationship. Heap it on, brother. And Jim didn't disappoint me.

We had a beautiful apartment. Jim urged me to buy whatever furniture I wanted. Nothing was too expensive. "Whatever you want, Pat." Allen had bought me very few gifts, and when he did buy a gift it was from the hardware store. Jim bought me *real* gifts, and not just on special occasions. On the way to his office he might see something he thought I would like in the window of a store. Later he would call the store and ask them to deliver it to my office. "If she likes it, I'll buy it," he told them. More often than not, I liked it.

Of course, he bought the best for himself, too—the best shoes, the most expensive suits, cashmere sweaters. He bought the car he thought was best and kept it immaculate.

Some days a big bouquet of flowers or a piece of jewelry would arrive at my office—more little reminders of Jim's love.

If there was a movie I wanted to see, he would drop everything and take me to the movie. If I wanted to try a restaurant, he took me without hesitation. Jim always wanted us to enjoy ourselves. Through all of our going and doing, I began to realize that Jim's emphasis was always on "us." *Just* us and nobody else.

"I don't see why you need anybody," he would say. "I don't need anybody but you. People are no good, Pat."

Before we were married I would ask, "When are we going to go out with people? When are we going to make friends?" Jim would always say, "We'll have friends after we're married."

But now we were married, and still we never went out with other people. And we never had friends come to visit. He made me stop seeing Paul and Theresa. As far as Jim was concerned, I wasn't supposed to have friends. There was no need for friends. I had him. I could go to lunch with people; that was business. But our private life was *ours* alone. He didn't even see the need for relationships with relatives. You visited them once a year because you *had* to.

There was one thing I hadn't discovered about Jim in our dating, "do-anything-you-want-to-do" days. But it was obvious now. Jim was addicted to television. The set went on when we came home, and it went off when we went to bed. Night after night we watched television. He insisted that we do it together, so he watched while I sat, bored beyond words. On the weekends, Jim's love for televised sports would fill up every available moment. He was *obsessed* by them. Many times we watched every single sporting event on TV; the set was on all day Saturday and Sunday.

When the sporting events were over and the TV finally was turned off, Jim would turn to another of his loves—progressive jazz. This was one more private world where he could withdraw and feel an unquestioned mastery. He had a fantastic collection of jazz recordings, some of them very rare. When he wasn't playing his own records, he would turn to a jazz radio program. He could identify each musician, and he knew who was playing what.

Beer always went with sports. Whenever there was

excitement, Jim brought out the beer. I didn't like what it did to him, but there didn't seem to be anything I could do to change it. When his attention turned to jazz, his drinking taste changed to bourbon. Jazz always seemed to depress Jim, and his continuous sipping of bourbon only deepened the depression.

After we were married I began to realize how much he drank, and I was afraid. I began to wonder if I really could live with it. Still, I reasoned, there were more good times than bad. And you had to expect *some* faults. Besides, we'd only just been married. Given a little time, things would get better.

CHAPTER 6

For Bitter or For Worse

It was Thanksgiving Day, 1969.

Thanksgiving is Pilgrims and harvest and turkey and pumpkin pie . . . and football—*televised* football from early morning until evening.

At our house it was generally football on TV and beer. But today it was going to be different. In just a little while we would actually drive out to the stadium to watch the Oakland Raiders. It was a cold, crisp, sunny day, and it felt good to be in the stadium instead of in front of the television set, to be around people and away from the tube.

I never really understood football, but the excitement of the crowd, the pageantry, and even Jim's excitement helped to make the afternoon warm for me. He was enjoying the game, and to my surprise I found myself enjoying watching Jim.

As I watched him I began to feel guilty. We shared so very little. Even a football game divided us. He enjoyed it while I endured it. Life was not very good to Jim, I thought. And slowly, quietly, something began to change inside of me that Thanksgiving afternoon.

It's good to be alive, I remember thinking. Jim really is

good to me. He's considerate—more considerate than I deserve.

The more I allowed myself to feel loved, the more my iciness began to melt. Down on the field a game was going on, unnoticed by me. In this part of the crowd, a quiet human drama was taking place. A woman was beginning to think of change. I began to imagine a new Pat, one who would soften just a little. We would have a quiet dinner in a little out-of-the-way place, just the two of us.

Jim would notice the difference. How surprised and happy he would be! He had wanted this for a long time. He had said it would happen, and at last it was beginning. After dinner we would go home for a quiet evening. We'd talk, get a little closer together—maybe even work out a few of the little problems that had marred our not-too-bad marriage.

In bed it would be different, too. Tonight he'd know I wasn't just going through the motions. I was going to try to respond, even if only a little.

The hardness was melting, and it felt good. What was taking place on the field was unimportant. The important action was inside me. Here was an event for the morning papers. A touchdown had just been scored in the name of kindness.

Dinner was a warm experience. Does Jim notice the little ways I'm different, I wondered? It isn't that much of a change, but wouldn't he catch any change for the better?

After dinner we went home. It was just a little after ten o'clock. In the car I sat just a little closer. Barely inside our apartment door, I could feel a smile coming up from deep inside me. I put my arms around Jim and kissed him on the cheek.

Knowing the answer, yet wanting for the first time to hear his response, I whispered "Do you love me?"

In a cold, icy rage he threw me to the floor.

"What the hell do you care?" he yelled. "You've never cared for me. Why do you want to know now? What have you been doing that makes you want to cuddle up to me now?"

He was standing over me. There was rage in his eyes. Then this broad-shouldered, muscular man reached down, grabbed me by my wrists, and jerked me to my feet. As he shook me, he reached back into a vocabulary I had never heard him use and called me every vile name he could think of.

He hit me in the eye, on the side of the face, and threw me to the floor again.

What followed was one solid hour of uncontrolled violence—violence so deep, so intense that I was pushed beyond any feeling of pain. Some unknown emotional reserve must have dulled my senses. Instead of pain, a feeling of raw panic began like a fire in the pit of my stomach and sent its electric shocks throughout my body. I wanted to run. Anywhere. Away. I had to get away from this maniac.

Several times I broke free, only to have him grab me and start the verbal abuse and the physical beating all over again. First it would be accusations. "You stopped off after work with business associates instead of coming right home . . . You did this . . . you did that. . ." Again and again he would accuse me, always coming back to the same few things. Then he would let go of one wrist and slap me furiously.

It seemed as if he would never stop. A look of hatred

and contempt—a look I had never seen before—seemed to be burned into the muscles of his face.

With each burst of his anger my panic mounted. Finally every fiber of my being said, "He's going to kill you." That thought brought with it a new burst of strength. I broke from his grasp, managed to get as far as the bathroom, and locked myself in.

Utterly exhausted, I sank to the edge of the bathtub. I was safe for the moment, but I still felt panic.

My breath was coming in deep gasps, like sobs but without tears.

I could hear Jim moving around in the living room. Slowly I relaxed. I could tell he wasn't going to break down the door. He was going to bed.

When I finally looked in the mirror I saw a beaten woman. Great bruises were beginning to show. Both eyes were turning black. My wrists were badly scarred. There was a red ring around my neck.

I turned out the light and sat down on the toilet, my head in my hands.

I had read about "battered wives" but I'd never known any. Now I *was* one. This had to be some wild imagination. Several times I turned on the light and looked in the mirror again, just to be sure this had really happened. And every time that same battered woman looked back at me. It *had* happened. That battered face was mine.

I ached all over. But I felt a deeper, more serious pain. I felt humiliated. People who beat their wives were skid-row types, I thought—drunkards. *Classy* people don't beat each other, and we are classy people. We may abuse people psychologically; that's acceptable. But not this real stuff. I was heartsick.

It was all so repulsive. If only I could run away, I

thought. I wanted to get out of the apartment, but I couldn't take the chance. Suppose Jim hadn't really gone to bed. Suppose he were only waiting to start all over again. Even if I *could* get out, where would I go? We had no friends. We didn't even know anyone in the building.

Wait a minute! Even though Jim hadn't let me see Paul and Theresa in months, I knew they would take me in. But I had no car keys. "Just sit, Pat," I said to myself. "You'll think of something."

"You asked for this," I reminded myself. "You knew better than to get married. This is not supposed to happen to cold, calculating people."

I thought, too, of Jennifer and Karen. What will they think of their mother if she's divorced twice? More than anything else I wanted them to look up to me. I didn't want them to be embarrassed or apologetic about their mother. Now, because of my stupidity, I stood a good chance of losing face with them, and I dreaded that possibility.

Sitting there as the long night wore on, I even thought of Allen. "You're partly to blame, Allen," I said to his memory. "If we hadn't been divorced, none of this would have happened."

Sometime toward morning I decided to take a bath. This was no get-ready-for-another-day bath. It was more like a desperate, emotional act of cleansing. I wanted to scrub away the pain and humiliation of that bitter, bloody night.

As I washed carefully, I thought of something that seemed to bring my whole miserable night into perspective. In the warmth of Thanksgiving I had broken my cardinal rule: Never soften. Be the user, not the used.

"You see what happens when you soften?" I asked

myself. "As soon as you showed any sign of affection, it was taken as a sign of weakness, and he took advantage of you. You've just learned a valuable lesson, old girl."

The pain lessened. The hurts were not so deep. I had found the steel that would keep me strong. Now I could face the enemy—I mean, my husband. Forget the warmth of yesterday, and hold fast to a cold, cold heart. Nourish that coldness.

I got out of the tub and put yesterday's clothes back on. An icy resolve was moving me now. There was no tug at my heart. I felt almost as if I had no heart.

It was morning, and I felt fearless. I walked out of the bathroom and right into the bedroom. Jim was still asleep.

I sat on the edge of the bed and jolted him awake.

He shook his head and rubbed his bloodshot eyes. He looked at me in disbelief.

Resting his head in his hand he said, "What happened to you?"

"You did this last night, right here in our living room. Just after we came home." I tried to piece together what had happened. But it was as if I were talking about someone else in some other place. He had no recollection of what had happened.

But he *had* to believe the bruises. Slowly he realized I was telling the truth. In his drunken stupor, he had totally forgotten.

Jim began to sob. Through his tears he pleaded, "I love you. I don't know what got into me. I don't know what I said, but I didn't mean any of it. I love you. I really do." And his voice trailed off, lost in his tears.

In my heart I said, "You can just suffer, Buster. You deserve the pain. Look at what you did to me."

Staring straight into Jim's eyes, I delivered an ultimatum. "Don't you ever do that to me again. Ever! I don't care if it's tomorrow, next week, or ten years from now. If you ever try to do that again, I'll leave you. Lay even one hand on me, and everything's over. Sober or dead drunk, it won't make any difference. Do you hear me?"

Still unwilling to believe what he was seeing, he nodded his head. I was cold as ice again. Jim liked me better this way. If he wanted nasty, then nasty was what he was going to get.

I got up from the bed, undressed, and then dressed a second time in silence. I wore long sleeves to cover my arms. A turtleneck blouse covered my neck. Heavy makeup disguised some of the facial bruises, but I still looked like a wreck.

Riding to work by myself, I concocted a story about an accident. "Jim and I had an accident," I told everybody. But nobody believed that story, and every time I told it I felt humiliated. Our car hadn't been damaged, so "it was a friend's car," I reported. All day long people came in and out of our office. And everyone wanted to know, "What happened to Pat?"

By the end of the day when Jim picked me up, I was fit to be tied. My anger from the beating was still smoldering, and now I felt a fresh surge of anger from having had to lie all day long.

From the moment I stepped into Jim's car that night, I was cold and guarded. What feeling I had had for Jim was gone for good.

Just as I expected, the colder I became the more solicitous Jim became. Morning after morning he brought me coffee in bed. When I stepped out of the shower he brought me a towel he had warmed in the oven. Every time I turned around, he was there to serve me.

I felt closed in. It was as if I were a prisoner in some idyllic jail. He was holding me captive by acts of love. It was more than just his way to atone for his "sin." It was emotional blackmail. Perhaps he felt that this would blur my memory, or maybe he was assuring me that the days ahead would be all sweetness. Whatever he was doing, it didn't work. I sensed that our Thanksgiving night would repeat itself.

I never kept less than twenty dollars in my wallet, just in case. And whenever Jim drank I put my purse right by the door, making sure my car keys and driver's license were in it.

One Saturday night Jennifer and Karen were with us, and we were going to a movie. Jim had been drinking beer and watching football all afternoon. I suggested that maybe he shouldn't drive. Like a shot he jumped from the chair and hit me with the back of his hand. Karen let out a little scream and ran to my side.

I said nothing. I didn't need to. Jim knew what I was going to do. I went straight to the bedroom, packed a few things for the girls and a suitcase for myself, and walked out.

I wasn't going back to that apartment, or to Jim. That was definite. Then I talked to him on the phone. This time it was, "I'll stop drinking. It's the drinking that makes me hit you." I didn't really believe he would stop, but I *wanted* to believe him. On Sunday afternoon I went home.

A job opportunity opened up for Jim in Las Vegas. He was excited about this new possibility. He didn't like the work he was doing in San Francisco. "The people here are dumb, Pat. That's part of my problem. Vegas will be different. The people there are smart. And Vegas will be fun. It'll be good for us." We moved.

One Saturday evening we'd been out on the strip gambling. Jim had lost some money, but not much. He was the kind of gambler who sets aside a certain amount of money to gamble with, and then doesn't go over that limit.

That night he was a sore loser. "Cut it out," I said. "If you lost it, you lost it. It's not the end of the world."

But he kept on. "What do you know about money and how hard it is to get? I buy you everything you need and want."

When we got home I put my purse by the door, just as a precaution, and went into the bedroom. I had just started to get ready for bed when Jim came out of the bathroom with fire in his eyes. He swung at me, but I ducked and ran for the door. I grabbed my purse, got into my car, and drove to a nearby motel. On Sunday I took the money I had and rented a small apartment. Then I called Jim. He pleaded with me to come back. "I didn't hit you. You said '*if* you hit me' . . ."

"Jim, this is the end. It's over—*for good.* I'm not coming back this time. I'm going to the lawyer tomorrow."

And I did.

I used the same lawyer as the first time. I was a resident now, so I only had to wait three days. The court procedure was the same mechanical five-minute process. I had the same, all-too-easy, after-divorce drink with the lawyer.

It was all over. The end.

I went home to my apartment, pulled the drapes, and shut out the world.

CHAPTER 7

Opening the Drapes

My world, the world behind the closed drapes, had stopped.

When the first marriage ended, I had staggered under the blow and run for family, friends . . . anyone.

Now it was different. A second marriage had ended. Inside I felt cold, numb, and out of touch. Here I was with a new address I couldn't even remember. Most of the furniture was someone else's. Everywhere I looked was the stark reality that seemed to scream at me, "You've blown it again, Pat."

The longer I sat in the darkness staring at the living room walls, the more my coldness gave way to panic. I felt as if my life were out of control. Something inside me ached for security and a sense of order, for someone to belong to. That's all I'd been looking for. Yet everything I tried turned out wrong—well, almost everything.

True—I'd kept my business life intact. There I felt competent and on top of things. In that world I was strong, even respected. The word had a good, strong sound to it. I was respected. People had told me so.

I heaved a sigh of relief. For a moment there was a flicker of light. And then the light went out. I was pretending. A satisfying career in the midst of a shattered life is *not* enough. You're kidding yourself, Pat. You want more than that. Much more.

My personal world was a wreck. Everything I touched turned to chaos. My relationship with Allen had ended. Then, with Jim, I had held back, and now that too had ended.

What did it take to build a loving relationship? Was there really any such thing? Or was I chasing some never-to-be-found pot of gold at the end of an illusive rainbow?

Just asking the questions seemed to give me a sense of quiet. These were the questions I should have asked years ago, questions I hadn't even thought to ask. I didn't have the answers. But even the questions felt good to me, and I embraced them. Quietly I began to look at the relationships in my life.

First I thought of Jim. That relationship was over. Yet I knew that mistake would scar my life for years to come. I couldn't help thinking of the things I would no longer have. The expensive clothes, the gold bracelets—I had loved those things. But they were only *things*, and I had paid dearly for them. Suddenly I saw that they had never been gifts of love. They were regular payments Jim had made on a property he was purchasing for himself. That's what had brought on the violence. But I had agreed. I was a property he owned, and since he owned me, I was his to do with as he chose.

With that realization, I knew I could do without the things. A sigh of relief rose from deep inside. I was no longer owned by Jim . . . or by anyone. I was free again. It was as if I were breathing cleaner air. I could have friends again. Oh, how I had wanted friends. I had been hurt badly when Jim had insisted that I break the relationship with Paul and Theresa—the only friends I had left. The only contact I had with Theresa before we moved was a brief phone call I had made to her from my office. A short time later, she had died.

In the vast silence of that little room, darkness settled inside of me. I thought of my father and my stepmother. There were no close relationships there. I thought of Jennifer and Karen. They didn't really need me. Their father could take better care of them than I could.

Nobody needed me. More questions came—dark questions this time. Why was I living? Why had I been born? Why did I need to continue this life? Why couldn't I just end it once and for all? What was I waiting for? I sat with my head in my hands.

"No. I can't do that," I said, snapping out of my suicidal despair. "I may not be able to put together a decent life for myself, but I will not take my own life."

In just a short time (was it minutes or hours?—I didn't know) I felt the exhilarating thrill of escape from the murky, darkness of suicide. I sat dazed, my mind blank. The darkness was leaving, but where did I go now?

You need God, a voice that had just popped into my head told me. *You need God.* There it was again. Where did it come from? "Who needs God?" I may have asked out loud. "God who?"

That strange thought would not go away. I turned from it to concentrate on getting my life moving again. Throw myself into my career, that's what I'd do. I began to make plans. I'd work sixty to eighty hours a week and really get ahead.

You need God, came the message again.

How could I escape this crazy idea? "I'll go swimming.

That will stop this nonsense." I opened my apartment door to the blasting summer heat of Las Vegas. I hurried to the pool and swam, hard and fast.

I lifted my head above water. *You need God.* I swam harder still. I was breathing fast. At the edge of the pool I surfaced to rest for a moment.

You need God. I couldn't believe it. What was wrong with me? Was I losing my mind? That must be it. On top of everything else that had happened, now I was going insane.

I had had only one religious experience in my entire life. Early in my marriage to Allen I had joined his church, a little Baptist mission. We became friends with Darrell, the young college student who served as pastor, and with Mildred, his wife. I could remember really liking them. We had good times together.

Then something had happened in the church. There was a big squabble. I can't remember what it was about, but I know that Darrell and Mildred were deeply hurt. And I was hurt because they were. I remember saying to whomever would listen, "If this is Christianity, you can have it. I have friends in bars who are nicer to each other than you are. I don't care if I ever see the inside of a church again."

And I didn't. That had been the end of the church stuff for me.

I went back to the apartment. I couldn't even remember what day it was. Something in my mind said *Saturday*. "Saturday," I said out loud.

You need God. There was that thought again. It would not go away.

I turned on the television and scanned the channels, looking for something—anything—that would occupy my mind. Nothing held my attention. There was no way to escape this unwelcome message. I sat down hard in the living room chair. I was angry now, tired of feeling pursued.

"All right. Stop it. I'll go to church tomorrow. I'll see if I can find God," I said, sure that whatever I was looking for, it was not God.

Defiantly, I announced to the stale air of the apartment and to any listening gods, "I'll go to the first church I come to. If God is there, terrific! If not, then we'll forget this whole God business."

Just as suddenly as it had come, the thought vanished. I sat there in the chair, expecting a rerun. But it was gone.

Slowly my mind relaxed, and I suddenly felt exhausted from the top of my head to the soles of my feet. I dressed for bed, and when my head hit the pillow, I fell sound asleep and slept like a baby through the entire night.

* * *

The warm sun was streaming through my window and I felt like a new person. I stretched, one of those absolutely delicious stretches. I was alive. The world was alive. I'd tapped some powerful new source of energy. The darkness of yesterday was gone.

Then in disgust I remembered my promise of the night before. It came back to haunt me. "I've got to go to church," I said aloud. Was that the reason I had slept so soundly? I had an eerie feeling that my promise and this new sense of energy were related.

"Well, an hour isn't going to hurt," I thought to myself. "I can do that. Who knows what might happen?" I showered, dressed, got in the car, and headed for church.

What would I do when I got there? Why did I feel so

compelled to go? "Never mind," something seemed to say. "You promised you'd go, so go."

Down one street and up another I drove, looking for a church. I would go to the first church I saw. Then I saw a steeple. That had to be a church.

It was a *churchy*-looking church. I parked, and as I walked toward the church I saw the sign on the front lawn: *Southern Baptist.* "I don't want this church. Of all the churches for me to pick, why this?" (Later I discovered I had passed three other churches on my way and had not seen one of them.)

It was too late to change my mind now. Awkwardly I pushed the door open. Two men stood at the door to the auditorium. I didn't want to see anybody. They must have read the look of angry determination on my face, because they started to offer me a program and then changed their minds. I marched past them, down to the third row from the front of the empty sanctuary, and sat down. I looked around. God wasn't there, so far as I could tell.

Suddenly a deep sense of futility swept over me. Once more I had put my hopes in something, and I had been let down. My *promise* had been a foolish idea. The longer I sat, the more foolish I felt. Five minutes till eleven. The longer I stayed, the more likely it was that people would come and talk to me. One thing I did not want to do was talk to anybody. I started to think about walking out. "Give me just a minute," I thought. "I'll get up enough courage to leave."

Just when I was ready to make my move, I heard a bell ring outside and the church began to fill. Hoping people would ignore me, I looked straight ahead. The look on my face must have said "keep away" loud and clear, because everybody avoided me. Although it was a crowded little church, I could have stretched out my hands on either side and not touched a single person.

Soon I heard a piano playing softly. Then a door opened in the front of the church. Into my line of vision walked Darrell Evanson—my friend from seventeen long years ago, the pastor of that little mission church I had left.

Somehow I *knew* God had done this. I couldn't explain it, but I knew it. A dam broke inside of me. All my years of pain washed across me at that moment, and with my tears came a sense of peace. It was as if some gentle inner voice was whispering to me, "I really am here. I *do* love you."

My eyes shifted instantly to the piano. It was Mildred, as I had so often seen her years ago. *Everything* was like it had been before. This church was larger, but it was built just like the little mission church. The piano was even in the same place.

I was struck with a deep sense of homecoming. A circle, begun seventeen years before, had just been completed. I didn't *think* that; I *felt* it.

Who knows what Darrell preached on that morning. It did not matter. I don't know if I stood when the congregation stood, or if I sat down when they sat down. I was overwhelmed. There is no other word to describe my feelings. I had come to find God, and, in a way I would never be able to explain, I knew I had found Him. But I had found something more. I was deeply aware that God had found me.

I don't remember what Darrell said at the close of his sermon, but when he finished I pushed past the people in my row. I was going up to the front to tell Darrell I had found God. I was going to see an old friend. I was going home. All at once. And I had to hurry.

At the altar Darrell recognized me and put his arms

around me. Oblivious to everyone else around, I poured out my story of the past few days and told him of the unexpected realization that I needed God. Through my tears of joy, I tried to tell him that now I knew there was a God and that God loved me. I was sure of that. Darrell listened without saying a word. He didn't need to speak; I needed someone to listen.

For the moment, all the memories of my seventeen years seemed to vanish. There was only the overwhelming, healing discovery that, in spite of my hardness, in spite of failing twice in marriage, God loved me.

It would be some time before I would understand what happened to me that morning, and still longer before I could even try to explain that experience. I only knew then that I had come reluctantly to find God, and that I had found Him. In finding Him, I had a deep sense of peace. This was the beginning of a deep inner healing, a new beginning. I knew it.

I had no sense of sin, no awareness of a need for forgiveness. I responded that morning to God's love and quietly opened my tangled life to His healing. There would be much to learn in the days and years ahead. But for now it was enough that God had invited me to come to Him and that I had responded.

I had begun a new adventure.

Still standing at the front of the church, I said once more to Darrell, "God loves me."

And he reassured me, "Yes, He *does*, Pat. He *really* does."

I think I flew home. Like a little child I was excited . . . giggling. Inside the house everything looked clean. The colors seemed fresh and alive. Had someone come in to freshen things up while I was gone? It looked as if someone had. Everything had a just-dusted look. Or was it that something had wiped away the cobwebs from my eyes?

As I tried to get in touch with my real world, I discovered that something else was different—my heart! That cold, steel box inside of me was warmer. Or broken. Or melting. I didn't know. In its place was the warm, feeling, caring heart I had always wanted.

The next morning I was at the church before Darrell got there. There was so much to learn about what had happened to me, and about what was ahead.

We talked for a while and then Darrell prayed for me. He prayed that God would continue to show me His love, that He would help me to know God's Son, Jesus Christ, and that I would commit my whole life to Him.

I didn't know then what that meant. But as he prayed, everything inside of me said, "Yes. Yes."

Then he gave me a modern version of the New Testament. "You'll be able to understand this more clearly," he said. He suggested a particular New Testament book I should read right away and gave me a study book that would help me to understand what I was reading.

At home I read. And read. And read. I couldn't get enough.

Again the following morning I beat Darrell to the church. I wanted to learn all there was to know about this new life. Darrell suggested another Bible selection to read and another helpful study book. He patiently answered my questions. Then I went home again to read.

On Wednesday morning I was back at the church with more questions. And again I left with a reading assignment. Day after day it was the same. I had found a boundless spiritual appetite. Sometimes I couldn't even wait until I got home to start reading my Bible. I would pull off the highway and start reading. This was food for me, and I was *so* hungry!

As I read, I began to see God more clearly. I began to understand why He sent His Son. I saw my need for forgiveness. And quietly, one day, I asked God to wash my life clean.

I began to care about people. I was less inclined to see them as things. It was as if I were meeting the people I worked with for the first time, and I was liking them.

The keypunch operator where I worked wasn't *just a lowly keypunch operator*. She was a person, a real person. She had a husband and a child. She had feelings.

To be sure, much of the old Pat needed changing. But life and hope were replacing darkness and despair. And my attitude had definitely changed.

In the midst of all this newness, I lost my job. I had been asked to do something I felt was unethical. I had lied before, in the days preceding this new life, but I couldn't let myself do it again.

I told my superiors I couldn't do it, and I was very direct. I told them I couldn't do it because I was a Christian. They were direct too. They threatened to destroy any future I might have in computer programming.

Their threats were real. Yet somehow, with strength that must have come from God, I still refused. I left with the feeling that losing my job had been a victory. And it had been. My former employer even paid off the balance of my contract. That payment gave me an income for the next few months and the freedom to pursue my search to understand more about God.

Jennifer and Karen were to arrive soon. They were going to spend the summer with me. I could hardly wait to tell them what had happened to me. Yet there was something in me that said, "*Don't* tell them. See if they notice anything. That will be the test of how real this whole thing is."

So I waited. Well, not entirely. I had to say *something*. I told them I had gone to church, just by chance. And just by chance, the pastor was a man I had known for a time in our early married years. Would they like to go with me? Sure. They would go with me.

I had begun to feel like a completely new person. But did God make the kind of difference people could see?

One night the answer came. Just as the girls were preparing for bed, Karen put her arms around my neck and said, "Mom, it sure is nice to see you so happy. You're different than you were."

"Thank you, Lord," I said inside. "This *is* real. They *see* it. Things are different. It isn't *just* emotion. Thank you, Lord."

CHAPTER 8

Instant Replay

Summer was almost over.

I'd been reading the Scriptures like they were personal letters written directly to me. No one taught me to pray, but I'd been praying simple prayers. Sometimes I talked to God about my concerns and fears, and other times I just bubbled over with excitement as I reported to Him what had been happening in my life.

My new life was only a few months old, but I could readily notice the softening. And I was aware of a keen new sense of anticipation about life. It was as if, piece by piece, God was putting together a new Pat. I felt so far removed from the old Pat. I had a new life.

I also had an almost-empty pocketbook. My money was running out, and I had to go back to work. There was no other choice.

"San Francisco—that's where I'll go," I thought. "I have a good reputation in data processing there. It'll just take a phone call or two, and I'll have a job."

But there was something else. For some reason I can't explain, I wanted to call Allen and get his advice. I was about to take a major new step. I was single again and starting everything from scratch once more. Maybe Allen would have some solid counsel.

I forced myself to reach for the phone and dial the number.

On the other end of the line his voice said, "Hello."

"Hi, Allen. Pat." I announced, as if he wouldn't recognize my voice.

"What's up?" he asked. "Do you need something?"

"Just advice this time," I answered quickly. I told him about my plans to get a job and move back to San Francisco. He listened to every detail without interruption.

When I had finished talking, Allen suggested, "Why don't you move down here to southern California? You would be close to the girls. They'd like having you here." There was a pause and then he added, ". . . and so would I."

I don't remember how I concluded the conversation. But I was stunned when I hung up. I hadn't expected him to say that.

I sat staring at the phone. Slowly the stunned feeling gave way to excitement. I felt like a little girl who had just talked to her first love.

"Was he really saying he wanted me close to him?"

"That's what he said," I answered myself.

". . . and so would I . . . and so would I," I repeated again and again, wanting very much to believe that it was true. "After all those years, something has happened. Allen's changed."

My mind was running wild with new possibilities. Did this mean that we might *see each other* again?

Still sitting near the phone, I talked out loud, half to myself and half to God. "Is this really possible? Is this something You're doing? Is this part of my new life?"

I already knew the answer. It was yes. Of course it was. A big, solid, resounding *Yes*. All the power of heaven and earth had begun to put my world back together again that night. I *knew* it. I wanted to leap for joy and I wanted to cry at the same time. This was more—*far*, far more—than I had expected.

Job prospects in southern California were terrible. I bought the Los Angeles *Times* at Las Vegas newsstands and read the classified ads. Jobs for programmers were scarce. I talked long distance to employment agencies that specialized in my field. They all told me the same story. The aerospace industry had slowed, and the Los Angeles market was flooded with programmers. They were pumping gas and parking cars.

One agency put it bluntly. "Don't come to southern California. Go back to San Francisco. Things are different there."

"But I'm coming," I responded.

"Then come prepared. You'd better plan on waiting at least two or three months. Can you afford to live that long without a job?" He didn't even wait for an answer. "That's how long it's going to take. It doesn't make sense for you to come."

"Sense? Don't talk to me about sense," I mumbled to myself after I hung up the phone.

Something else was at work here. But there wasn't any way that the agency man could know that. This was a very special secret that only God and I shared.

I called Allen with my progress report. He had an answer.

"Listen, this is what you can do. Remember the apartment at the clinic? It's small, but nice. I used to live there. Now that I have the townhouse, it's vacant. You can live in that apartment until you find a job. It won't cost you any money."

It was almost more than I could have asked for.

I packed up and headed for southern California. I *think* I remember driving. But inside I was floating. Flying home. It was part of a miracle.

When I arrived, Allen had decided I wasn't going to live in the apartment at his clinic. He had another solution. "It would be better for you to live in the townhouse with us."

I couldn't believe my ears. I had felt all along that I was coming home. But everything was happening too fast. This was more than I ever could have dreamed. While my insides jumped with excitement, I listened to Allen's plan.

"Everything will be on the up and up, Pat. I have a full-time housekeeper. She lives in. She'll be like a chaperone. I've already discussed it with her. See, there are four bedrooms." He was showing me the townhouse. "The housekeeper has one. Karen has one. Jennifer has one. Then the master suite is mine. You'll stay in Jennifer's room. When you get a job, then you can get your own apartment."

Over and over my heart said, "Now we'll be close enough to rebuild the relationship. No, I don't want to rebuild anything old. I'm a new person. Allen will see that. He *has* to see that. We can build a completely *new* relationship."

I moved in. The girls were delighted—especially Jennifer, because we shared a room. I was delighted. And—miracle of miracles—Allen was delighted.

During the days I went job hunting. In the evenings, Allen and I spent hours talking. We talked about things that had happened years before.

"Remember when we had three dollars left, and I wanted you to take me to a movie?" Yes, Allen remembered. And we talked. We talked about all the little things that should have been long forgotten, but instead had been stored away in the musty closets of our memories. So many hurts were replaced by understanding and forgiveness. Something beautiful was happening between us.

Allen suggested that I get involved in the singles program at his church. "And," he added, "we want to give our new relationship time. I think you ought to date. And I should too."

My heart didn't agree, but my head said he was right. I dated halfheartedly. And I felt hurt when Allen dated. I reminded myself that our relationship would take time.

One morning I was down in the kitchen fixing coffee. The girls had gone to school, and the housekeeper was away for the day. It was Allen's day off, and he was sleeping late. As I sat down to drink my coffee, Allen came downstairs. He gave me a playful, innocent kind of kiss. Soon that kiss was followed by another. And another. Before long we were in bed together. This was my man, and I was back with him, sharing the most intimate of moments.

After that, we found other times for intimacy, and in that intimacy I felt reassured that I loved Allen. It was more than the pleasure of sex.

It wasn't until some time later that I saw that my rationalizations were wrong. What we were doing was a sin.

After almost two months, I found a job. Then I found an apartment across from the girls' school. The move was right, I sensed. Allen and I were growing back together, but it *would* take time. Those weeks so close to him had been great. Maybe now I needed to slip away and let him miss me. We'd still be together, but not as much.

Late one evening in my apartment I was sitting on Allen's lap. "You know," he said softly, "sometimes it's all I can do to keep from saying, 'Let's go get married next weekend.' But I really want to make sure it's the right thing."

Increasingly we were talking of remarriage. All was right with my world. I had every reason to be filled with joy. God was in my life. Day after day I was discovering life-changing truths in the Scriptures. I had found a childlike freedom to play, to just have fun, because my life was being undergirded by the solid rock of Jesus Christ. I had found the source of life, and it was a joyful, bubbling stream.

As the year progressed, my faith deepened. At every turn in the road God seemed to be providing me with food for spiritual growth. The ugliness of my past life was being cleansed. Old ways of doing things, ways that displeased the Lord, were being forgiven. God was changing my values. Life had become more than the status apartment and the fancy car I once had. Now my apartment was simple, and I drove a Volkswagen.

I was beginning to develop some honesty. When God made me aware of a needy place in my life, it was painful. But more and more I was able to admit my need and ask for God's help. Less and less I resorted to the old excuses, "After all, Lord, my father was a . . ." or "My mother was a . . . What do You expect from me?"

All during that good year, that year of growth, I dated Allen. My dream of remarriage was very much alive, but I kept it to myself. "Things like this take time," I reminded myself again and again. "No need to have everybody talking about us and wondering when it's going to happen." Somehow, keeping our times together as secret as we could made them more special, more *ours*.

Once we were driving home from the desert. I felt peaceful, an inner kind of quiet. In the stillness I became especially conscious of the way God had been changing my life. Deep inside I felt warm . . . and grateful to God. I reached over and put my hand on Allen's leg. In almost a whisper I said, "I feel so refreshed. All those old things that happened to us, I hadn't realized how they had poisoned my life. All those fears. The anger. The frustrations. They were ruining my life, Allen. Sometimes I can look back at the way I was and" (it hurt to say it, but I had to), "I can begin to understand why you wanted a divorce."

My eyes were getting misty. I could feel the warm beginnings of tears of joy in the corners of my eyes.

"I tried to change back then, Allen," I continued, "but I just couldn't do it. Now God has changed all that. I can't get over this feeling of being new . . . on the inside."

As I thought to myself of some of the ways I had changed, even in just the last few months, I felt Allen stiffen.

"Sometimes I feel uncomfortable around you, Pat. You're so different from me. I don't think you would be happy doing things with me. I'm not so sure it would be wise for us to marry again."

My joy vanished. I felt cold. My only response was a pained silence. I said nothing to Allen; there wasn't anything I could say. But my heart prayed desperately, "Please God, can't we both walk to the middle? Can't You change us so our lives fit together?"

We drove the rest of the way in silence. Our goodnight kiss was gentle, but noncommittal.

As I knelt by the side of my bed I wept uncontrollably. I hurt so deeply that it was almost physical. I clenched my fists until my knuckles ached. Then I shook my fist at God. At first it was a wordless kind of anger. Then, through my tears, I yelled, "Is this what all the changing was for?"

My tense, aching arm fell to the bed, and I buried my face in the blankets. Finally my anger quieted, and I crawled into bed. As I lay there, over and over again I remembered Allen's words: "I'm not sure it would be wise for us to marry again." *I'm not sure . . . I'm not sure . . .*

Finally I fell asleep from sheer exhaustion. But in the morning the pain was still there, and it stayed for many mornings to come.

Slowly, things returned to near-normal. The first summer of my new life had now stretched into a full year. Then it was a year and a half. I had the best of all worlds, for sure. My job was going well. I was growing spiritually. There were lots of good times with the girls. Allen and I were still dating. Those were good times. There was not as much "Let's-get-married" pressure as there had been. But that was healthy, and things were *good* between Allen and me. Whenever he called and wanted me, I was there. My dream was very much alive—quieter now, but still very much alive. I was keeping myself for Allen.

During the Easter school break, Allen took Jennifer and Karen to Lake Havasu in Arizona. This had become a family tradition. Loaded down with a tent and what seemed like enough camping gear for thirty people, they left, pulling the boat.

I missed them, but I told myself they were having a

great time. Anyway, I couldn't be with them even if they *had* asked me. I had a job to do. I couldn't leave.

On Tuesday of that week I got a call from Allen.

"Pat, I want you to be with us. Can you take the rest of the week off?" He didn't wait for an answer. "I'll pay for your plane ticket. You can fly to Las Vegas and then on to here. The girls and I will meet your plane. We'll drive home on Sunday, and you can be back at work Monday morning."

It was as simple as that. With my heart beating wildly with excitement, I quickly agreed. "Sure, I'll come."

I almost ran to my boss's office. This was not one of those "could-I-please-have-time-off" situations. I announced that I would be gone for the rest of the week. "I've just had a phone call from Allen. He wants me to be with him." My boss knew my heart was already in Lake Havasu, and he agreed to let me go. The other people in the office caught my excitement too. Nobody complained about my leaving so suddenly.

I caught the first plane for Las Vegas and spent the night with a girlfriend. Early the next morning she put me on Puddle-Jumping Airlines for the flight to Havasu. The plane had two engines and only eight seats—but I felt as if I were riding a magic carpet. Couldn't the plane fly any faster? *My family wants me to be with them,* I felt like shouting—to the pilot, to the winds, to anyone who would listen.

Allen, Jennifer, and Karen met me at the little airport. We hugged and kissed, and I heaved a sigh down deep inside that said more eloquently than words ever could: "It's good to be together."

Quickly we loaded the supplies, the tent, the sleeping

bags, and the water skis into the boat and headed for our own spot on the far shore of the lake.

What a great week it was. We cooked out, and the food was delicious. The water was so cold we could hardly stand it when we fell in. "Helps to keep you on the skis," we all agreed. The nights were magnificent. The heavens were freshly splashed with a million stars . . . just for us.

When we played, we played hard. When we slept, we slept soundly. The sheer joy of that week seemed to wash away the years we had been apart. Everything we did said, "This is a family. This is the way we were meant to be."

All the months of waiting were worth it . . . for this.

Then, before we knew it, the week ended. We loaded the car, hitched the boat and trailer, and headed back for southern California. We drove through the night, keeping ourselves awake with coffee. Early on Easter Sunday we arrived back in town. A brilliant yellow sun followed us into the city.

Allen dropped me off at my apartment, promising to pick me up in time for the evening candlelight service. We were going to church together as a family. He kissed me good-bye.

I took a long, luxurious hot shower, washing away the dirt and dust of a week in the outdoors. But I held on to the memories of our togetherness, savoring each delicious recollection.

In the late afternoon I awakened from sleep, buoyed by a feeling of peace and tranquility. The desert sun had gotten deep beneath my skin. I felt warm to the very core of my being.

That Sunday evening was special. The four of us

trooped into church as a family. We were together again, united now at a deeper level than we ever had been before.

This was the miracle I'd been praying for but had hardly dared to believe could really happen.

The next days were busy ones. I had so much to catch up on at the office. That meant extra hours at work. And there was laundry to do. But the week had been so good that even washing load after load of clothes couldn't dampen my spirits.

Allen had been busy, too. Everyone had waited for the vet to return, and he had to work late into the night to take care of their animals.

Wednesday evening Allen called. "Pat, will you come over? I want to talk to you." Nothing more. No explanation.

"Of course, Allen. I'll come right away."

"What could be so important?" I wondered as I hurried to my car. I felt a tinge of apprehension. I repeated his words in my mind, studied what I remembered of his tone of voice.

"It's nothing," I told myself. "Forget it."

When I arrived, his housekeeper announced, "He's upstairs in his room. He'd like you to join him there."

The coldness in her voice washed over me as I climbed the stairs to his bedroom.

Allen was propped up on his bed. He motioned for me to sit down. There was no welcoming kiss, and we exchanged only the barest of pleasantries. The warmth of the past week was gone. Something had happened; I could feel the chill of it. Quickly Allen got to the point.

"You've met Sue, my bookkeeper at the clinic."

"Yes," I responded.

"Well, she's decided to divorce her husband and . . . I want to marry her."

It was as if someone had hit me on the head with a blow meant to split a log in a single swoop.

My world went blank. I felt my living, breathing heart turn icy cold. Off in some distant shadow I could still hear Allen's voice.

"She's been vacillating. She's tried to make a go of it, but it isn't working. She's been through a lot, and she's done more than anyone could ever expect. At first I admired her—respected her, I guess. Finally I realized that I love her, and I want to marry her."

I sat in stunned silence, trying to shut off my feelings. But that old control was gone. I knew he could read my heart.

Finally I got enough control to say, "Allen, we've been dating for over a year. We've talked about remarrying. We've just spent a great few days together. Was all of that a lie? This thing with Sue didn't just start since we got back. It must have been going on for a long time. Why did you lead me on? Why did you let me believe we could make it? You knew all along it would end this way."

"I didn't know it would end this way, Pat. Sue has gone back and forth between staying married and divorcing Phil. I figured if she didn't leave him, I'd marry you."

Down came that great axe for another blow. This was worse than the first. I'd been kept in reserve. I was a back-up, a fill-in.

I remember getting slowly to my feet and walking to the door. Allen was saying that he and Sue had some things to work out yet. I walked calmly down the stairs and got into my car. I started the engine and drove home.

Gripping the wheel tightly, I tried not to think. Above all, I tried not to feel. I just wanted to get home.

CHAPTER 9

Starting All Over Again, Again

On the trip back to my apartment my mind was like a camera, taking intense three-dimensional pictures of every little scene . . . a small girl, dressed in white, standing under a street light . . . a very stocky woman and her child . . . the colors of the cars.

None of the things I remember so vividly were important to me at all. Yet my mind was snapping these mental pictures, filing them away as if I would need them someday. Some deep urge for self-preservation was at work, keeping me from having to think about what was *really* going on inside of me.

When I reached my apartment, I got ready for bed like I had on a thousand other nights. It was only nine, but I got into bed.

I sat, propped up, staring straight ahead. There were no tears. I couldn't cry. I didn't talk to God. There was nothing I wanted to say to Him.

I stared at the wall. An hour or more must have passed, and still I stared.

The phone rang. A voice invaded my wasteland. It was a friend, Richard, calling to talk about a Bible study class.

In the middle of a sentence he broke off. "Pat, did I wake you up?"

"No." My voice was emotionless and cold.

"O.K. About the class . . ." But he sensed something. "You don't sound right. What's happening? Something *is* wrong."

"No. Everything is O.K., Richard," I lied easily, but unconvincingly. "I'm just tired. What were you saying?"

"Pat, I don't want to pry, but I'm going to. Whatever has happened, I feel like you need to talk about it, and I'm ready to listen."

That was all I needed. I *had* to talk to someone.

"Richard, I went over to see Allen this evening. He called and asked me to come. And when I got there. . ." Suddenly, without a moment's warning, my cold inner wasteland became an intense, raging battleground. I spat out my anger, not at Allen, but at *God.* Feelings came pouring out like the rapid fire of a machine gun. My dream had been shattered. No. It was more than *my* dream. *God* had given me that dream. And He had put my family back together again. I was flooded with the now-bitter memories of the past week and of Sunday night . . . all of us walking down the aisle as a family.

Now God had taken all that away. He had put it within my grasp, only to snatch it away again. He let me see how good it tasted just so He could take it away.

"God betrayed me, Richard. God let me down," I mumbled through my tears. "Here I am, alone and humiliated. Do you know what that feels like, Richard?"

"Of course I do, Pat. You know that. But you're not alone. You're *not* alone." Richard kept trying to make me hear that. But I wasn't willing to hear. There was too much anger yet to be spewed out, too much of the battle's fire left inside of me.

Richard broke in again. "Pat, think about this."

"No." I spat back at him. "I don't want to hear more."

"Listen to me. God allowed me to call you tonight. He let me be with you in your pain. He *does* care. God will only be in control of our lives when we give Him permission. It may have been God's will for you and Allen to remarry. But if it wasn't Allen's will, if Allen didn't give God permission to control that part of his life, God wouldn't force him to marry you."

Then Richard added something I didn't want to hear—something I couldn't believe. "God can even bring good out of this, Pat."

"How could good come from *this?*" I began to sob. The violent anger was subsiding. I wept uncontrollably. Richard was trying desperately to assure me of God's love. I heard what he was saying, and more than anything I wanted to believe that God could bring good out of this. But I couldn't. And I couldn't stop the tears.

As long as I cried, Richard stayed on the phone. Sometimes I heard him quoting the Bible. "Lo, I am with you always, even unto the end of the earth." Other times I just knew he was there, caring.

Finally I went dry; there were no more tears. I was exhausted and the phone was like a dead weight. Richard suggested I get some sleep. I told him I would try.

I put the phone down, lay back on the bed, and quickly fell into a sound sleep.

Next morning I awakened late, feeling as if I had been drugged. My eyes were swollen and puffy, and I ached all over.

I called my office to say that I wouldn't be in. It was an effort just to dial the phone.

I lay back down on the bed, exhausted. Sleep would have been a blessed relief, but it wouldn't come. My eyelids were heavy, but my insides were already beginning to churn as I relived the bitter events of last night.

I'd been beaten again. That's what had happened. This time there were no bruises, no marks or scars. This beating was all on the inside. Allen had taken my hopes, my dreams—all that I thought we had going for us—and he had smashed them into a thousand pieces.

I was just beginning to taste all over again the bittersweet memories of our good times when the phone rang. It was Richard again.

"Pat, you must be feeling down," he began. "I know *you*. If you were O.K., you'd be at work." Then, with a special sensitivity in his voice he said, "You shouldn't spend the day alone. I want you to get up and have lunch with my daughter and me."

"I don't want to do that," I protested. "I don't want to leave the house." Right then I didn't think I could tolerate having lunch with a five-year-old.

"You've got to, Pat. I'm not going to take no for an answer." He sounded as if he really meant it.

Resenting his demand, I muttered, "Maybe I will, and maybe I won't."

"Either you do it, Pat, or I'll come over and throw you into the shower and get you dressed."

The idea that he might just do that was almost funny, funny enough that my tension broke, and I relaxed just a little.

"All right, I'll come."

"If you aren't here in an hour, I'm coming to get you." And he hung up.

I dragged myself out of bed and started to get ready.

When I met five-year-old Christina, my arguments melted. She was like a fresh spring breeze, a precious gift from God. Immediately she took me into her busy little world. She reported to me the latest news on ladybugs and mean older brothers.

Christina captured me and hauled me off to her special world. And I loved it. She didn't ask about what had happened to me, or why I was having lunch at her house. She just accepted me, and in minutes we were old friends. She shared her treasures with me. In a whisper, she told me her deepest five-year-old secrets.

Just for a moment I closed my eyes. Something was melting inside of me . . . just a little bit. Unbeknownst to her, she was working a gentle miracle. She was softening my hardened heart.

I felt a tug at my hand. "Pat, Pat, are you sleeping?"

"No, Christina. Only thinking."

"Oh, yah," she chuckled. "Daddy does that sometimes. Well, c'mon with me. I want to show you something else." And we were off to see another wonder.

The three of us had lunch in a lovely, quiet setting overlooking a formal Oriental garden. For a while no one talked. Christina broke the silence. "You look sad."

"I *am* sad, Christina. I don't really feel very good."

"Oh, I'm sorry," was her only response. Then we all went back to eating.

I drank in the stillness. Christina's gentle ways were touching me deeply. Through her I began to see God's love again. As bruised as I was, I could not deny that love.

Everything inside me was still aching, but I knew I was surrounded by God's great love.

Allen had rejected me in that parking lot years ago, when he had refused to let us try to put our marriage together. And now he had rejected me a second time. I had never felt such deep disappointment.

I tried to hold on to my disappointment. Darkness had fallen on my life so many times before. I wanted to grip at the anger and feel its bittersweetness.

Yet, in spite of myself, I knew I was going to be all right. There *was* light, even in this darkness. "Lord," I protested, "I don't want to start all over again." But no sooner had I thought those words than I knew that was *exactly* what I had to do. And with that realization came the sense that I *could* make it. God was going to walk with me through this darkness. This was not going to be the end.

"Are you sure you're not sleeping?" It was Christina again.

"No, Christina. I mean, yes, I'm sure I'm not sleeping. I'm sorry."

"Oh, that's all right."

After lunch Richard talked to me. He repeated again what he had said over the phone. He talked patiently but insistently of God's ways. "Something good will come of this, Pat. Just wait and see. God will do good. I know He will."

Richard said it, and I knew he was right.

But it was Christina who made me believe it.

Together they gave me a beautiful gift of new hope that day. I began to believe that good *could* come from this. I didn't have the faintest idea what it would be or how it could possibly happen, but I didn't need to know right then.

Again and again in the days and weeks ahead, the pain would come sweeping across me like a scorching hot wind. But as I left after lunch that day I had a quiet assurance of God's love.

In the car on the way home I caught myself singing. I don't remember the song; it was enough that there was *any* song for me to sing.

My mind drifted to my apartment. Mentally I walked through its drab, undecorated rooms. "You need to do something to that apartment," I said to myself. It *was* drab. After all, I hadn't planned to live there very long.

"Why not trim it up a little?" I remember thinking. I stopped at a furniture store and found a bookcase that I liked. In my mind's eye I could see just the place for it. I'd move a piece of furniture or two, put the desk over there, and move the lamp here.

Could I really be a little excited about going home? It was strange that God could so quickly begin to restore order. I bought the bookcase and headed for home. No sooner was I inside the door than I could see other things I needed to do. A picture needed to be hung. I needed something new for the bathroom. This was actually going to feel like home.

Then, slowly, the warmth of God's love, the warmth that had brought hope to my dark valley, began to fade. On the outside I was still doing all the Christian things I'd done before. But inside, that cold wasteland returned.

My old anger was replaced with a new kind of anger. *They* were to blame. Allen and Sue had ruined my life.

Jennifer and Karen told me about everything they

knew that was happening. And I let them do it. I encouraged them to report to me. I was seething with anger, and I wanted to feed its ugly flames with every little tidbit of information I could find.

The girls resented Sue and I smiled inwardly at their resentment. Sue tried to develop a relationship with them. I gloated when they rejected her efforts.

My bitterness and resentment cropped up in every conversation I had with Allen. He had sowed the wind, and now he would reap the whirlwind of my wrath. I would see to that.

Allen went to great lengths to involve Sue in every aspect of his life. She was always around. I couldn't avoid her. When she called to make arrangements regarding the girls, I spit at her over the phone.

My anger was coming from a deep, seemingly inexhaustable well. Yet through it all, I prayed earnestly for the hurt to stop hurting. I hoped (and even prayed) that Allen and Sue would break up. I saw every problem between them as a ray of hope. Their relationship *was* going to break up.

As a way to handle my constantly churning emotions, I worked extra hours. Sometimes I worked eighty hours a week, seven days a week. There were even weeks when I worked a hundred hours.

In the midst of all this, there was one small bright spot on my horizon. An attractive widower worked in the office with me. Jack was interested in me and often came into my office to talk during the day. We had lunch together. He was always supportive. He really seemed to care about me.

While my anger toward Allen deepened, I tried to hold

a piece of my emotions for Jack. I needed love and support now more than ever. And Jack must be God's answer to my need, I told myself. Jack would take Allen's place.

But despite my frantic efforts, my life was going nowhere. The pieces weren't fitting together. My career, the one thing in my life that had always sustained me, was going downhill fast. No matter how many hours I worked, I wasn't accomplishing anything. My boss was frustrated. "When are you going to get your part of the work done, Pat?" he asked me.

Other business associates, people I had trusted, began to ask the same questions. I felt defensive. Surely they could see that I was putting in all kinds of extra hours. What more could they expect of me?

No matter how hard I tried, I wasn't getting anything done. So I worked even harder. Physically and emotionally exhausted, I could feel my world crumbling. But still there was Jack, my replacement for Allen.

In the space of just a very few days, however, even that part of my world crumbled. I discovered that he was not the caring person I thought I knew. In fact, he was a fraud. I found out that he *had* been widowed, but that his wife had died because he had refused her medical care. And there was another wife and two children he had not told me about, and $10,000 of unpaid alimony and child support.

Once again I had grasped at some small ray of hope, only to be humiliated and hurt.

"Lord, I must be some kind of emotional casualty," I thought. I was totally unable to make any kind of decision regarding men. And I certainly wasn't able to determine God's will.

"Why in heaven's name do You speak in a still, small voice?" I asked God. "I need you to yell at me. Couldn't You call me on the telephone just to make Your will clear? Or You could write me a letter and say, 'Pat, today I want you to do this, this, and this.' "

I was staying with Betty, a friend from church. I tried to share my feelings and fears with her. One whole weekend we talked and talked, but I began to feel like I was beyond help.

Monday at the office I got a phone call from my father. Dad didn't call often. My stepmother was about to have brain surgery, he said. He seemed to be reaching out to me, asking for help without really saying the words.

"Why this now?" I screamed inwardly. "I can't take any more!"

I wanted to reach out to Dad. I wanted him to love me, and I wanted to love him. I felt like he was saying he needed me. And without a doubt, I needed him. More than ever before, I was a little girl that needed a daddy, and I couldn't reach out to him.

I mumbled some words into the telephone. That was all I had to give. And I hung up.

Later that afternoon I felt a chill. I put on a sweater, but the chill persisted, and worsened. I began to feel sick. My temperature went up. At about seven I left the office and drove to Betty's home.

Betty looked up when I walked through the door. "You're sick," was her only comment. She put me into bed in her bedroom immediately and took my temperature. It was 104. She called the doctor. It was just the flu, he assured her, and prescribed some medication.

I *was* sick. But I knew what I had was more than the flu.

This had to be an emotional thing. I was losing my mind. *That's* what it was: I was losing my grip on life.

Somewhere around eleven that night, at the height of the fever, I told Betty I knew I was losing my mind. "All this turmoil is more than I can handle."

Betty had not expected this, but her response was instantaneous. She sat down on the side of the bed and took my hand in hers. As she gently stroked my forehead, she said quietly, "Pat, God has not given you a spirit of fear, but of power and of love. He has given you a sound mind."

Again and again she repeated those words. Her voice seemed to cut in and out of my consciousness, but it was always there. Sometimes she made me repeat that Scripture verse, a phrase at a time.

And all the while she gently touched my head or my arm.

Hours passed, and still Betty kept repeating the Scripture, holding onto sanity for me when I couldn't seem to hold on for myself.

As the clock crept toward four in the morning, Betty tried once more to get me to repeat those words, "a sound mind," but the quietness of God had finally taken over. At last I had fallen asleep.

CHAPTER 10

Changing

"I did it again, Betty. Allen rejected me, and I jumped into another weird relationship. Why do I do that?" I asked as I brushed the sleep out of my eyes the next morning.

These were questions I should have asked years ago. And I wasn't really asking Betty for answers; I was asking *myself*. She knew that; she sat silently on the edge of the bed, listening.

"I'm a neurotic woman. I'm sick. Mentally sick." The painful admission came out slowly. And yet, saying it aloud brought a sense of relief.

"You need help, Pat. Why don't you go see Dr. Anderson? He's a Christian psychologist." There was a quiet insistence in Betty's voice. Dr. Anderson had been a gift from God when Betty's husband had asked for a divorce. I had heard some of the story.

"I'm going to call him," she said, not waiting for me to agree.

A week later, on an extended lunch hour, I found myself in Dr. Anderson's office. Walking through the office door had been difficult. Waiting, I had wondered if I really needed to be there. This was a place for sick people—*really* sick people.

Then I sensed an inner quiet. I felt washed by a wave of honesty. This was a place for sick people, and I was one of those people. I was right where I should be.

In a few moments a door opened and a big, warm-looking man with a generous smile said, "Pat, I'm Dr. Anderson." Something about him made me relax. It wasn't hard to see that he was a man who cared in a kindly, grandfatherly way.

In that very first session, I began to tell Dr. Anderson my story, the *whole* story, even the details I had never shared with anyone else. His quiet way made me trust him, and that trust allowed me to open my life.

He represented the possibility for deep healing, not just superficial calming. Perhaps he could reach down into hidden places and untangle the tightly knotted emotions that were killing my relationships and destroying me.

Don't misunderstand. I found that there was a big difference between *wanting* to be fully open and actually *being* open. Lots of times I wanted to pull back, to keep some thought or feeling to myself. But I came to understand that a memory that painful was crucial to the process of healing. So I forced the words out—sometimes in tears, sometimes in anger. But I got them out.

Therapy wasn't a game for me. It was life or death. I gave it everything I had, and ultimately it proved to be a major turning point in my life.

There was another reason why I threw myself so intensely into therapy. This reason was not as lofty as the desire for emotional health. But it was there, and it helped drive me to find wholeness. Underneath the pain, underneath all the garbage, I suspected there was a salvageable, "neat" person. When I found her, Allen was going to see her. And when he did, he was going to be very sorry he had rejected that "neat" person. Maybe he would be sorry enough to change his mind and come back where he belonged.

There was time. He and Sue weren't married yet. I still saw Allen. He would ask me to come over to talk about our girls. And every time he called, I ran. I wanted him to call. I wanted him to be dependent. The more he needed me, the more he would see the new me and the more he would want me instead of her.

I kept on praying, "Lord, don't let him marry Sue. Let him have his little romance. But then break it up, Lord." And I would end my angry, vindictive prayer with pious thoughts such as, "After all, this is really Your will, Lord."

Somewhere in the process of praying and grasping every opportunity for Allen to see the new me, another light broke through my darkness. Allen *was* going to marry Sue. Nothing was going to change that. It seemed as if God began to tell me to get on with the business of becoming whole. "Live your own life, Pat. Not Allen's. Not Sue's. Not anyone else's. Live your own life." Deep inside of me the message became clearer day after day. "Stop trying to make things happen. Stop looking to Allen for your fulfillment. Start living again. Become the person *you* were meant to be."

Slowly I found I could draw away from Allen. Many times he called to say, "I need to talk to you. Why don't you come over?" More and more often my answer was, "I really don't have time to do that. Why don't we just talk on the phone?" Sometimes I was able to say, "Allen, that's a problem you will have to solve. I can't answer that for you." Then, hurriedly, "I have to go now," and I would hang up, leaving him with no opportunity for argument.

Gradually I was able to turn my focus away from Allen. It certainly wasn't quick or easy, but it *did* happen. And somewhere in the process of therapy I divorced Allen internally. I'd had the legal papers for years. Now I had the far more painful, far more final, internal divorce. Yet in the pain there was a deep sense that at last I really could begin living again.

Week after week I went to Dr. Anderson. And week after week I talked, reliving the past. I was shocked by the bitterness and anger that so often rushed uncontrollably to the surface.

As I thought of the things my father and stepmother had done to me, hot tears of anger burned my cheeks. "My father never loved me," I blurted out. "Mother died having me, and my father blamed me for her death. He holds me responsible. That's why he's never been a *real* father."

On and on I raged, spewing out one hurt after another.

"And that horrible woman, Dr. Anderson. She hated me. She told my father all those lies about me. I hate her, Dr. Anderson. I hate her!

"I married Allen to get away from her. He was the only boy I dated that didn't like my stepmother."

As the weeks went by, it seemed as though I peeled away one layer of anger only to find still another layer underneath.

"Pat, when are you going to forgive your father and your stepmother for what they did to you?"

"What did you say, doctor?" I heard the words, but I couldn't believe them.

"When are you going to forgive your father and stepmother for the things they did to you?" he asked again, slowly and deliberately.

"Do you know what you're asking?"

"Pat, *I'm* not asking you *anything*. It's not my question; it's *God's*."

He reached for a Bible, found the page, and read, " 'For if you forgive men for their transgressions, your heavenly Father will also forgive you. But if you do not forgive men, then your Father will not forgive your transgressions' " (Matt. 6:14,15, NASB).

"Can you understand, Pat, that part of your illness comes from an unforgiving heart?"

"But Doctor," I said condescendingly, "you haven't been listening to me all these months. It's my father and my stepmother who should be asking *my* forgiveness. I haven't done anything to them. *They* did those things to *me*." I was crying now. "They did them to *me*. Do you understand that? *They* should ask my forgiveness. *I'm* the one with the screwed-up life."

Again there was a quietness in Dr. Anderson's voice. "Yes, Pat, that's probably true. But we aren't talking about *their* mental health or *their* accountability to God. We're talking about *yours*. That's all we can deal with. Just *you*. Not your father or your stepmother.

"For weeks you've told me that you hate your stepmother. Can you see the need to talk this over with God and ask His forgiveness?"

My face was dark. Puzzled. Hurt. I didn't want to hear what Dr. Anderson was saying. I had good, solid reasons for my hatred. Couldn't he see that?

Just weeks ago, when I had begun this process of therapy, I had hated myself. Then slowly I had seen how self-hatred was destroying me, and I had begun to change. I was a long way from really loving myself, but I was doing better. In the process, I had begun to see what my father and stepmother had done to me, and gradually they had become the objects of my hatred. They were the guilty ones, and they *deserved* my anger.

Yet there was something inescapable about what Dr. Anderson had said. I had to keep trusting him. Now was not the time to quit.

I decided to try to pray for my stepmother. I didn't begin with much enthusiasm. On my knees, I said, "Now, I want to pray for my stepmother." The words seemed to sting as I said them. I couldn't go on. As I continued to kneel, my mind began to bring up the hateful things she had done to me. In just a moment or two I was feeling dirty, repulsed by the whole process. I got up from my knees in disgust. This was not the way to healing.

But it was. Again and again I tried to pray. And slowly it began to happen. I discovered that the willingness to forgive is not something that drops from heaven in one big lump. Instead, it was a process of growth. My ugly "prayers" began to give way to more real prayers.

For the first time I saw my stepmother as a person with real hurts and pressures. I was beginning to understand that God loved me in spite of my failures, in spite of my ugliness. And if that were true for *me*, it had to be true for *her*. She *was* forgivable.

I remember the night that fact came clearly into focus for me. It was on one of the rare Sunday evenings when I was able to pull away from work to go to church. During the service, the pastor asked if there were any special things for which the church could pray. As people began to talk about needs I felt an urge to ask for prayer for my stepmother. My old anger said a loud, "No! Don't do it."

With a battle raging inside me, I stood. When it came my turn to talk, I said simply: "My mother is very ill. She has an aneurism on her frontal lobe. We are afraid she is going to die. Please pray for her." I began to cry softly. I continued to stand for a few moments, and the tears flowed from deep inside.

When I finally sat down, I realized what had happened. I had called her "my mother." I had called her "mother" before, but only when I *had* to. Tonight I had said it, by choice, in front of 150 people.

There was something else, too, in what I had said. "We're *afraid* she is going to die." Not long ago, when I first heard she was ill, I had thought to myself, "I hope she dies."

God had brought me a long, long way. While the service went on around me that night, I was lost in a very private world, a world of gratitude to God for what He was doing in my life.

* * *

"Pat, be good to yourself. Resign. Find another job. God doesn't intend for you to kill yourself because of some misguided sense of duty." Dr. Anderson had heard my job frustrations, and now he was suggesting a way out.

I was still working fourteen hours or more each day, Saturdays and Sundays included. But I wasn't accomplishing anything. I seemed to be on a treadmill, running continuously but getting nowhere.

I could feel my boss's disappointment. He had heard great things about my skill as a programmer. The project I was working on shouldn't have been a problem.

I was tired of working. Every day was an effort. I was

exhausted before the day had begun. But I couldn't leave the job. I had promised to help finish a new computer system. I heard what Dr. Anderson said, but I had some weird need to punish myself with a job that was a colossal failure. I could not leave.

Jennifer and Karen came to see me one evening, but their visit was no social call. After we exchanged hugs, I could see something was bothering them.

"O.K., guys. What is it?"

Karen spoke for both of them. There were tears in her eyes.

"What are you doing to yourself, Mom? We never see you any more."

I started to interrupt to explain, but she kept right on.

"When we do see you, you're so exhausted that we hate to talk to you, 'cause we feel like you ought to be sleeping instead of talking to us. Why don't you quit?"

"Yeah, Mom," Jennifer broke in. "Why don't you?"

I didn't have an answer. But I started thinking. Their questions, coming on top of Dr. Anderson's probing, gave me the courage I needed to think about quitting, or at least about taking a first step toward finding a new job. I called a "headhunter," a friend who was a professional job finder.

Before long my friend called with some news. The Broadway Department Stores were interested in me.

"It's the perfect job for you, Pat. They need a project manager to work in merchandising systems. I've already told them about your retail experience, and they're anxious to see you. Can you make it tomorrow?"

The interview was great. I was just the person they were looking for. It seemed to be a gift from God. I would be doing what I had been trained to do, things I had always done well. On top of all those good things, I would have weekends off.

"Yes, I'll come. But there's one thing. No, two. I need to give notice at my present job. And my mother is critically ill. I need to spend time with her. I'm not sure when I can come."

"That's fine, Miss Chavez. We understand. Will you call us in a few days to tell us when you could start?"

"Yes. Oh, yes. I'll call." I think I walked three inches off the floor as I left the personnel office.

The next day I gave my employers two weeks' notice. But they had something else in mind; they suggested I leave right away. That hurt, but I could understand their position. Besides, it took the pressure off. Now I could visit my mother and dad.

I left immediately for the desert to see my parents. One evening when I visited the hospital's intensive care unit, I stood at my stepmother's bedside, looking down at her still body.

"She's so old and grey. So shriveled," I thought. My father had lived with her for thirty-four years. As far as my relationship with her was concerned, those had been bitter years, lost years. The sadness of that fact washed over me.

I reached out to touch her. I was searching for some way to let her know how sorry I was, some way to say "I love you" after all these years. She opened her eyes, but she stared unseeing, unrecognizing.

"Please, God," I prayed, "don't let her die now, just when I want to love her."

That prayer was answered . . . "no."

In a few days Dad called. "She's gone," he said. "She died just a little while ago."

"I'll be right there, Dad."

"No, don't come tonight. Wait 'til morning. Get some rest, and come in the morning."

"Dad, I'm coming now," I insisted. "I'll be there as soon as I can."

He didn't object.

As I hung up the phone, I was sad. I could feel pain at her passing, yet there was beauty in that pain. Only a few short weeks ago I would have felt relieved. Instead, I was feeling pain. And I could say, "Thank God." It was a sign of the healing God was doing in my life.

There was something else I heard in that conversation, too.

My father needed me. He didn't say it in so many words. He was too self-reliant for that. But there was no mistaking the message in his voice. He needed me.

As I drove the sixty miles to his home, I prayed, "Lord, could we begin again? After all these years, could my dad and I build a relationship? Help me to hold on to You. Let me be a source of strength for him."

In the days that followed, I watched my father mourn for the woman he had loved so long. I saw him slowly accept the reality of her death. And I felt him reach out to me for strength.

One day I overheard him talking to a friend on the telephone. The friend must have offered to help, because Dad said, "No thanks. Pat is taking care of everything."

Something leaped inside of me in that moment. To anyone but me that would have been just a casual comment. But I had listened for those words all my life and had never heard them.

In my early years my father was "away." I made my grandfather into a father. Then, when I did go to live with my father, he seemed to have standards I could never meet. I did everything I knew to earn his approval, but nothing worked.

Dr. Anderson had helped me to see that I didn't need to perform for anyone. "All your seeking for approval, even the endless hours of work, tell me that you're looking away from God to other people and things for fulfillment. Fulfillment and peace come from God, Pat. They're like the water Jesus spoke about. They're *in* you now. They have to spring up from the person of Christ dwelling in you."

His words were not new, but I *really* heard them for the first time. They helped bring an end to my struggle for approval.

A few weeks later, Dr. Anderson and I both realized that the therapy was over. The process of growing would continue, and no doubt there would be crises down the road. But I had taken giant strides toward emotional health, and it was time for a new step.

As I left his office that day, it was hard to believe that only five months ago I had come to this office fearing that I was losing my mind.

One by one, I recited to myself the things that had happened. I had remembered the painful memories. I had cherished the insights and savored the joys. I had felt the good feeling of growth.

I was overwhelmed with gratitude to God.

One step at a time He was building a new life, and the process of re-creation was good.

I woke up one sunny Saturday morning feeling very much alive. I had a tennis match scheduled, and I was anxious to get out on the court.

Right there in bed, breathing in the goodness of the

day, I began to thank God for all He was doing in my life. In the midst of my joy and gratitude, I realized that something in me had changed in just the last few weeks.

"I don't have to get married!" I fairly shouted.

I shook my head. I couldn't believe it. After all this time I had finally accepted my singleness as a gift of God. I could actually accept it with joy. Whether singleness was to be a permanent state or not, for *then* it was right.

I began to realize that for a long time I'd been in some kind of holding pattern, poised to enter the mainstream of Christian living as an exciting, vibrant, lively woman . . . as soon as I got married. I'd become a victim of "when" thinking. *When* I have someone with me, then I'll lead that Bible study. *When* I have my new home, I'll do this or that.

My needs had not changed. But now I felt free to pursue love, not marriage.

That simple discovery made people more comfortable with me. They were no longer pawns to be maneuvered into better playing position. They were people—the men *and* the women. Slowly my relationships became richer as I saw people in a new light.

I didn't take a vow of celibacy. I didn't stop dating or enjoying the company of men. But a quiet contentment began to work its way into my busy life. And best of all, I began living more in the *now* and less in the future. What a change this was in my approach to life!

It was some years later that I sat by my father's side in his hospital room. For quite some time I had known he was dying of cancer. And I'd had the deep satisfaction of really loving him.

We had always lived so far apart. Even when we had

been close geographically, there had been hundreds of miles between us emotionally.

With the nearness of his death I realized how much I needed him, whether he needed me or not. I threw reserve to the wind and just loved him. We didn't talk about the pains of the past. I didn't sense the need for that. Nor did we talk much about the fact that I wanted a new, loving relationship. It was enough that he could *feel* that something had changed. A lot of explanation just wasn't necessary.

A few small words became a part of this new relationship—words like "I love you, Dad."

We'd never talked like that before, and it was especially difficult for Dad. The first few times I told him I loved him, there was a painful silence. As time wore on, his response became a mumble. I read it as "I love you, too, Pat," but no one else would have known he was saying *anything*.

Finally, he could bring himself to say "I-love-you." Those words sounded like a symphony to me. I was willing to go on loving him regardless of any response to my expression of love. By now I knew he loved me, whether or not he could say it. But hearing it, after all those years, was sweeter music than I had imagined.

I visited him often in the hospital. As the cancer spread, many times he slept through most of my visit. But we were together just the same. Quietly I held his hand. For reasons I can't explain, the slate of my memory was washed clean in those days with him. I knew he had not always been a good father, but I couldn't remember *why* he had not been a good father. The fact remained: He was a good father now.

Sometimes I sang to him—old Mexican songs that he loved and songs I'd heard him sing and play years before. Occasionally I sang Christian songs. He couldn't sing with me anymore, but his eyes lit up when I sang. He still had a melody in his heart and the feel of guitar strings on his fingers.

In the past few years my dad had become a Christian, a quiet, determined kind of Christian. There was not a lot of talk about it; that wouldn't have been Dad. But I could see signs of his faith.

When it came to the cancer, Dad was a realist. That was the way he wanted it.

One evening I came into his room with my usual, "How are you, Dad?" His response was direct.

"How on earth do you think I should be?"

"I guess you're feeling pretty sick."

"Well," he responded quickly, "that's how I am."

"Dad, I'll pray for you. I think God will give you strength."

"Oh, I 'm going to be all right. I made up my mind today that I'm going to be an invalid, and I'm not going to live very long. Up until now I thought I was going to get well. I was planning on getting out of here and going back to playing some golf."

"No, Dad, I don't think you're going to do that."

I couldn't tell him he was going to be well again. Our relationship was too honest for that.

Not long after that, I drove the seventy miles to the hospital to visit him before leaving for a business trip. We laughed together that night, more than we had for some time. When it came time to leave, I told him I loved him, and bent down and kissed him. We prayed and then I left quietly.

CHANGING

During the night he died.

Another chapter of my life closed that night. Like so much of my life, the last pages of that chapter, the richest pages, had been written with words and acts of love. Tenderly, we had closed the book together.

PART II

PITFALLS AND POSSIBILITIES

CHAPTER 11

So You're Thinking of Divorce

Twenty/twenty hindsight is a fairly common commodity. Many of us can see clearly what we *should* have done.

Every now and then, as I've grown stronger since that dark Sunday and my first divorce, I've wondered what would have happened if my response to Allen had been different. What if I had simply *refused* to leave? I've thought often of what I might have said.

"You move out if you want to. I'm staying right here. Six months from now, if you still want a divorce, we'll talk about it. Right now, this is my home. This is where the children belong, and I'm not going to leave. What I did was wrong. I admit that. But you're going to take some of the responsibility, and I'm going to stay."

Recently I suggested to Allen that I could have taken that direction instead of simply packing and leaving. His response was quick and direct. "We'd probably still be married if you'd done that." And I agreed. That would have forced us to work through some of the problems, instead of making major decisions under the emotional pressure of that painful weekend.

Exhaust *All* the Possibilities

Let's talk about you for a moment, starting with the possibility of reconciliation. Here is a basic principle I've given to men and women all over the country: If you have any choice at all, *don't divorce.* Despite what people may tell you, the life of the formerly married isn't all that glamorous.

From the midst of a chaotic marriage, the single life looks peaceful and glamorous: no more nagging, no more frustration, and a whole new world of freedom.

Just ask a divorced person. Nine times out of ten he'll tell you what you want to hear. "Hey, listen. Get out of that marriage. Let me tell you about my life. I can go wherever I want to go and do whatever I want to do. Nobody tells me what to do."

But be careful. Much of what you're hearing is shaped by feelings of guilt and disappointment, and the feeling that life hasn't really been all that good. Instead of saying "I blew it," a divorced person concocts a story to sell the rest of the world on the supposed joys of singleness.

When people consult me I say, "Don't do it. Let me tell you what this life is really like. Dating again sounds great, doesn't it? Well, it's not all that much fun. More than likely you'll get into a new relationship very much like this one. If you don't have yourself together, if you haven't learned how to handle life, each new relationship is going to be just as painful as the one you're in right now. In your present relationship, you at least know what the problems are. Isn't it better to try to work out known problems than to run away and exchange them for more of the same, *plus* unknown problems in a new relationship?"

With men, I talk about the problems related to children. "The children are probably going to resent you at first. After all, you left them.

"On the weekends you may pick up hostile, hurting kids. And you won't really have the time it takes to work through their hostility. If you *do* try to work through it, chances are you'll tell them that their mother is partly to blame. But they don't want to hear that from you, and they shouldn't.

"So more than likely you're going to avoid that whole area. Instead you'll play 'Superdad.' You'll take them to all the places you never took them before. You'll do the things you always meant to do, but never did. Unintentionally you'll teach them to expect you to spend money on them—lots of it.

"And there's something else. If you have children, you're going to continue to be in a relationship with your ex-mate for a long, long time. Decisions will have to be made about the children and property and financial obligations. Instead of working out those details as partners, most likely you will have to negotiate them as adversaries."

"What's it *really* like to be divorced?" a businessman asked me. After hearing my response, he moved back home with his wife. "We've got to work these things out," he told her. "The truth of the matter is, I want to move out, but that isn't a very good answer. Let's try again." They were able to put their life back together.

As we worked late one night on a computer, one of the other programmers asked me about divorce, and I gave him the whole story. When I was finished he said, "You're the first person who's told me *that* kind of story. Everybody else has said what a neat life it is."

When he got off the computer at three in the morning, he went home and awakened his wife. "Get up, honey," he said. "I've got to talk to you. We're not going to get a divorce. We're going to get some counseling and straighten things out."

That was an ultimatum, but fortunately she heard it as, "I care enough about you and our marriage to do what it takes to put it back together again." They got into counseling, and they did put the marriage on solid ground.

I don't want for a moment to suggest that all marriages can be salvaged. But I do want to urge you to *try*.

The easing of our divorce laws has made divorce more humane, more compassionate, and less vindictive. But in the process, divorce also has been made an easier, more available option for families that *do* need to try again.

Dr. James Kilgore has written a book called *Try Marriage Before Divorce*. At first I thought that was a strange title. Then I realized that in one simple phrase he was saying the very same thing I am: Exhaust every resource you can ("try marriage") before you settle for a split.

While every marriage will not be saved, nothing is lost by trying again.

The Ultimate Help

Whether your marriage can be salvaged or not, *you* certainly can be. The pieces *can* be picked up. And despite the dark fears you may be facing right now, there is light . . . and hope.

I'm not talking about a whistling-in-the-dark kind of hope. I mean *hope. Real hope.*

It's not hard to imagine what you are feeling at this

stage in your life. Whether you are just beginning to lose your grip on your marriage, or if it has already slipped through your fingers, you can't help feeling unloved . . . and perhaps even unlovable.

Nothing creative can happen in your life until that feeling changes. Until you feel loved . . . genuinely, deeply loved, you're going to feel inferior. Insecure. Fragile. And you're probably going to lash out at others—just to protect yourself.

But I said there was hope. And I meant it. When everywhere I turned my world was loveless, and everything inside me cried out that I didn't deserve to be loved, help came from an unexpected Resource, one I didn't even know was there. Quietly, yet very clearly, God let me see that He loved me . . . just as I was. Somehow He broke through my pain and mental panic to help me know that He understood what I was feeling and hadn't rejected me.

Please don't dismiss this as glib, pious God-talk. Out of my own experience I could not offer you any more realistic, more concrete, more genuinely helpful advice.

Go to God. Pour out your pain and your anger. As simply, as directly as you can, tell Him what you are feeling. Let it all out. He won't be surprised or shocked. Then, as the anger subsides, allow Him to let you know how much He loves you, and how much He wants to love you into a complete recovery from this difficult experience.

If this idea is utterly foreign to you, let me back up a step or two. Maybe you have only some vague idea that "out there somewhere" there is a "higher power." Or perhaps you don't have any feeling that God *is* . . . or that He's interested in you at all. Let's begin there. As an experiment, try a very simple, very honest prayer. "I don't know if You're there. Are You? If You are, I need help."

There's no hypocrisy in that request. It's straight and direct, and I believe it is a plea that God will answer.

It's not a very formal prayer. But it is a beginning, a crack in the door that can allow God to begin to work in your life, showing you His love and putting His great, limitless resources to work for you.

Pray that prayer consistently . . . daily for one week, two weeks, or even a month. Treat this as a serious experiment, and you will begin to find help from God.

Seek . . . and you will find help. God can be found standing at the door to His love, the door to new life and hope. He wants very much to help you find the door.

Years ago, Rev. Samuel Shoemaker described that door as

> . . .the most important door in the world—
> It is the door through which men walk when they find God. . .
> The most tremendous thing in the world
> Is for men to find that door—the door to God.
> The most important thing any man can do
> Is to take hold of one of those blind, groping hands,
> And put it on the latch—the latch that only clicks
> And opens to the man's own touch.
> Men die outside that door, as starving beggars die
> On cold nights in cruel cities in the dead of winter—
> Die for want of what is within their grasp.*

A second step in prayer is to ask God for forgiveness. Not only for the things you have done—or not done, but most of all for not accepting His offer of love and forgive-

*Helen Shoemaker, *I Stand by the Door* (Waco, Tex.: Word Books, 1977 [reprint]).

ness earlier. As you open your life to Him and seek His forgiveness, know that He *does* forgive. Even when your mate, your family, or friends cannot or will not forgive, even when you cannot forgive yourself, God forgives through His Son, Jesus Christ.

For me, my new life began several years ago with the surprising news that God loved me. The very idea staggered me. It was hard to believe. Yet, the more I allowed myself to sense the reality of God's love, the more *I* began to change. It didn't happen all at once. I wasn't zapped by instant wonderfulness. I didn't become an overnight mystic. But I began to understand that I had become God's child, the child of a loving Father. I began to feel that He was bigger than my problems. I knew I had found *the ultimate Resource.* And with these new realizations, I could react to my ex-mate differently. I could see my destructive attitudes more clearly, and in very practical ways, those attitudes began to change.

Recently I was rushed into a hospital intensive care unit with a pulmonary embolism. I had been recovering from surgery, only to have *this* happen. I was angry at everyone around me, *including* God. When I tried to pray the only thing I could say to God was, "I know You are there. I know You love me, and I love You. But I don't want to talk to You right now." And that feeling lasted for several days.

Finally, on a Saturday morning, I was lying in my hospital bed, still unable to pray, still wanting to tell God how angry I was at Him for my illness. Somehow, God broke through my anger, and I was made deeply aware of His love for me. Then, I found myself thinking of all the performing I had done in my life; working first to please my father, then working to please my husband. As I began to feel the frustration of all that effort, it was as if God said ". . . and you've been performing for Me. Stop it. I love you, even if you never do another thing for Me. You can't earn My love. I just love you."

I heard no voice, but my anger and frustration melted before the warmth of God's love. The realization that I was loved, regardless of any effort on my part, was the beginning of a long road of recovery for me. Things really changed from that point on. And they can change for you.

I don't have a formula to give you. Things won't work for you exactly as they did for me. But God's love and His help *are* real. And they are continual. They keep on working, changing you, moving you toward a richer, more meaningful life.

People sometimes say to me, "You're the most 'put-together' person I know, Pat." And almost inevitably, when they say that, I'm feeling anything *but* put together. I'm convinced that people see me as a person who continues to open herself to God's love. Not a perfect person, but a growing person.

Even in the "pits" of life, God seems to give me a sense of deep joy—a joy that sustains. The deeper down you get and the more external resources you have exhausted, the more that joy is the only remaining resource. The more you realize your limitations, the more God's joy becomes a powerful life-changing, situation-changing resource.

Trust the *ultimate Resource.*

Seeing a Counselor

Everyone knows counseling success stories. Everyone also knows about counseling failures. There is no magic in counseling, no guarantee. It can succeed for those who are willing to work at the process of discovery and growth.

Counseling can only help when both parties are serious about wanting help. If only one person sees the need for help, counseling can help him or her, but it won't necessarily help preserve the marriage.

While we want to hold on to hope as long as possible, we must also be realistic. Counseling has the best chance of success if it is begun *before* the marriage has seriously deteriorated. Effective counseling teaches each partner to hear what the other is really saying and feeling. Those skills are best developed when the partners are not severely threatened and can learn to develop a reasonably non-defensive posture. If those conditions cannot be developed, counseling will not be effective.

A Christian counselor needs to help both parties to rely on the Holy Spirit and take responsibility for changing *themselves*. In the beginning, most people want to establish guilt—the *other* person's. Counseling can help when each party is willing to get beyond guilt and accusation and to deal with his or her own needs.

Whenever some discovery hits close to home, it's a natural tendency to say, "If only my mate could hear this." In reality, that response means that this is almost certainly something you need to hear. You could be right—your mate *may* need to hear it. But don't let your mate's need cloud the fact that the only response you can control is your *own* response.

Jesus said, "Why do you look at the speck of sawdust in your brother's eye and fail to notice the plank in your own? How can you say to your brother, 'Let me get the speck out of your eye,' when there is a plank in your own? You fraud! Take the plank out of your own eye first, and then you can see clearly enough to remove your brother's speck of dust" (Matt. 7: 3–5, *Phillips*).

Without mutual commitment to discovery, change, and growth, no amount of counseling can help, and the hope you may have held on to for so long must be allowed to die.

Sometimes, even *in spite of* that commitment to change, little can be done. In some marriages there has been so much pain, and feelings are so solidified, that one of the parties finds it less threatening to start over again in a new relationship. With a mate who knows all your weaknesses, you are vulnerable to hurt.

Love and a sense of support encourage change. But where there is no love and little or no sense of support, there is no climate for change. A person who sees the need for change may have so completely cut himself off from the love of his mate that he feels he must find that love in another relationship.

Looking for a Counselor

Here are some simple guidelines to help you select a counselor.

1. Get recommendations from a pastor or someone you trust.
2. Don't choose a friend as a counselor.
3. Don't select a counselor who has previously counseled either of you.
4. Make a preliminary appointment and then decide together whether you can work with this counselor.
5. When you decide, be as open and honest as you can with the counselor. Nothing is gained by holding things back.

6. Make counseling a top priority, and be prepared to work at it.
7. Even if your mate decides to quit counseling, continue for your own good. A change of counselors at this point seldom increases the chances for preserving the marriage, and if you continue, at least you'll be honoring your own commitment to growth.

Remember, divorce is rarely a solution to a troubled marriage and is, at best, a tragic last resort. Exhaust all the possibilities.

CHAPTER 12

The First Few Pieces: Children, Lawyers, Settlements

When a divorce takes place, there are several areas that need to be addressed at once. These include:

- telling the children
- finding a lawyer
- arriving at a fair settlement (including alimony, child support, and child custody)

But let me begin this chapter with an area of consideration often overlooked: understanding the specific *causes* of divorce, the ways marriages die. In fact, I'm putting this fourth area first because it helps determine how you will deal with the other three matters introduced above.

1. Try to Understand Your Own Divorce

For most of the years of human history, a wife took care of the family and provided the things necessary to survival. The home was her domain, and its care was her responsibility. Outside the home was the husband's territory.

In ancient times, he defended the home and family. In more modern times, he worked to provide money, cared for things outside the home, and ruled the family. Those survival demands required most of the energies of a married couple. Marriage had a host of very practical, very useful purposes.

In recent history, the need for survival skills has greatly decreased. And with that decrease, new pressures have been placed on marriage. Increasingly, marriage must be intimate rather than simply practical. It must fulfill each partner's needs, satisfying expectations of companionship and meaningful sex, rather than simply being useful.

Tevye's question in *Fiddler on the Roof* reflects these changes.

"Golda, do you love me?"

His wife replies that for twenty-five years she has washed his clothes, cooked his meals, cleaned his house, milked his cows, and given him children. What could be more proof of love than that?

But Tevye is still not satisfied. He asks again, "But do you love me?"

Exasperated, Golda recites even more of the things that prove her affection—such as fighting with him and sharing his bed. "If that's not love, what is?" she implores.

Sheer survival has kept them together. But now Tevye is searching for something new in the marriage. And he concludes, "Then you love me?"

"I suppose I do . . ."

"And I suppose I love you, too."

Very few couples are content to come to Tevye's and Golda's conclusion based solely on the things one does for the other. Even today, many couples are held together by crisis and by the demands of family. But when they survive the crisis, they begin to ask Tevye's question. And, increasingly, the answer is "I'm not sure."

In many marriages, each partner's emphasis is increasingly on self-fulfillment: "What do *I* need? What's good for *me*?" As a result, there is less desire to subordinate personal needs to the needs of another or to the needs of the marriage—the two made one.

These are the pressures that increasingly lead to divorce.

A Single Overriding Problem

Some see divorce as the result of one overriding problem or event, such as alcoholism, gambling, money problems, or another man or woman.

Inevitably, the ex-spouse is seen as the villain. This is a trip back to the Garden of Eden. The first human family knew how to judge the *other person* completely at fault. "The woman you gave me, she gave it to me," Adam said. "She is at fault, not me," is the clear message.

Let me say some brief words about a "third-party situation." Often a girlfriend or boyfriend seems to offer a problem-free relationship. The grass on the other side is *so much greener*. But often these are not long-lasting relationships. Maturity and a willingness to forgive *can* bring restoration to a marriage that is torn by adultery.

Incompatibility

The second, and perhaps most common, reason for divorce is incompatibility. One partner is perceived by the other as not meeting his emotional and sexual needs. Or, in a more frivolous vein, the tastes and habits of one partner are an irritant to the other. Here again, the ex-mate is most often the villain. "It's his fault (or hers)."

No-fault Divorce: Growing Apart

There is one last type of divorce. It could be called the "drifted-apart divorce." No one partner is at fault. There is no strong feeling of hatred, but rather an agreement to part. The partners reason that either the marriage was a mistake in the beginning, or they don't have enough in common to stay together. "Let's shake hands and call it quits."

* * *

The *ways* in which marriages terminate also vary. One song tells us there must be fifty ways to leave your lover. Let me mention the obvious two.

The Sudden Breakup

For some, a seemingly good marriage erupts into a demand for a divorce. The strong feelings of one partner surface one day and come as a surprise to the other. One partner may come home to find the other packed and gone.

As a rule, the remaining partner is in need of emotional ear surgery. His or her hearing has been seriously impaired. This partner has completely missed the other's distress signals. Although counseling may not bring the absent partner back, the "surprised" partner owes it to himself or herself to learn some new listening skills.

The Slow Process Breakup

For most divorced couples, however, there is time between the first serious talk of divorce and any action to initiate proceedings.

This was the story in my marriage to Jim.

In such situations, partners frequently alternate between making verbal or physical attempts to destroy each other and pleading "I'm sorry" as they make some effort to repair the relationship.

Each quarrel seems to end well. It produces some sense of healing and leaves the partners with the encouraging feeling that they have now found an answer to their problems. What follows most often is an attempt to show *excessive* courtesy. Remember the heated towels and the coffee in bed after Jim beat me?

As this pattern continues, one party finally decides that nothing has changed and nothing is *going* to change. Divorce seems to be the *only* answer.

Just knowing where you fit into the pattern of divorce is not tremendously helpful by itself.

It *is* helpful if it gives you some insight into why the separation happened. It can help you see yourself a little more clearly, and that could be a first small step in recovery.

It can also help you feel that you are not alone. Even though no two divorces are exactly alike, knowing that your separation is not *all that different* can give you one small shred of sanity to hold on to while your world falls apart.

2. Telling the Children

There isn't any nice and easy way to do this, but let me summarize the things to keep in mind: I'll deal more with this throughout the chapters that follow.

a. *Be the first to tell them.* You don't want them to overhear it in a conversation or hear about it from someone else.

b. Children have a tendency to feel responsible for the divorce. In simple terms, try to explain to them what has happened. This isn't going to be easy. But be quick to explain that the divorce is not their fault; *it is a problem the parents haven't been able to work out.*

c. Don't put your children in the position of having to choose where they will live. *You and your ex should make the choices.*

3. What About a Lawyer?

Before you see a lawyer—and you should see one—you should understand that a lawyer . . .

- often can encourage divorce. Many have no moral commitment to save a marriage.
- may try to force you to move too quickly.
- can keep tempers high.

Now that you've looked at the dark side, let's consider how to choose the lawyer you want to represent you. Don't be afraid to *shop for a lawyer.* And be sure to ask questions on the very first visit.

- How many divorces has he handled?
- What percentage of his practice is divorce cases?
- What are his fees? Remember that you are going to pay for every bit of his time that you use.
- What are your rights under the laws of your state?

Attempt to determine whether or not you are going to be able to trust this lawyer. If you're not satisfied with him or his answers to your questions, pay him and look for someone else.

When you finally select your lawyer, don't blindly put your life in his hands. Responsible lawyers encourage you to make your concerns clear. If something doesn't seem right to you, question it. Don't be afraid to disagree.

Attempt to work out as much as you can with your ex-mate before you reach your lawyer's office. Once your lawyer is negotiating with your mate's lawyer, and especially once matters must be settled in court, you've stopped communicating.

While it's much easier to suggest than to practice, try to maintain goodwill. Check your attitude. Why are you suggesting this or that? Is this really the best in the long run? Are you trying to get revenge? You'll live with the results of these attitudes and actions for a long time, so take all the time you need to determine what is really best.

4. What About the Settlement?

Don't expect the court to make your new life for you. Be prepared to make it on your own as much as possible, no matter what the court says. Even though you're faced with a thousand problems, if you allow yourself to be defeated inwardly now you'll be a long, long time recovering.

In the very beginning, recognize these basic problems:

- You probably are not going to be able to maintain your present life-style.
- It is rare for a court to order more than $500/month child support, unless a husband's income exceeds $3,000 a month. Courts consider that the husband may soon have a second family to support.
- More than half the child support ordered by the court is never paid.

- Don't expect the court to *make* things happen or prevent things from happening. The courts may order, but they are relatively powerless to force or prevent actions.

With these thoughts in mind, I suggest that you consider the following options in your attempt to settle the most difficult areas in a divorce action.

Alimony

Against my lawyer's advice, I chose not to ask for alimony. I knew I could support myself, and I did.

This may not be possible for a woman who must try to re-enter the job market. But it should be a goal. You should be free from depending on your ex-mate as soon as possible.

While we're talking about money, let me offer this suggestion about spending. Often a woman feels that now she must have a new wardrobe, and a car, and the list goes on and on. The rule to remember here is to spend only what you absolutely have to. This is an uncertain time, so don't load yourself down with debts that will only add to your frustration.

Child Support

Since I didn't ask for alimony, I was free to concentrate my money request on the children. Here, too, my lawyer wanted me to demand a specific figure. But I felt that if the judge ordered a specific amount, Allen would be inclined to pay *only* that figure. I wanted him to face more responsibility than that.

We agreed that he would accept financial responsibility for the girls. He has been totally responsible, much more than any judge would ever have ordered.

Of course, my situation is just that—*my* situation. Yours may be vastly different, but I urge you to operate on the premise that, as much as is humanly possible, the husband is primarily responsible for the financial needs of the children.

Child Custody

Contrary to popular opinion, divorce is often harder on older, rather than younger, children. But children *can* adjust to divorce.

When deciding matters of custody, bear in mind these things:

1. Try to separate *your* needs for the children from *their* needs.
2. A child still needs both parents.
3. Determine which living environment is best for the children.
4. Disrupt a child's sense of security as little as possible.

Unless the other parent physically or emotionally abuses the children, you ought to consider establishing joint custody of the children if at all possible. Another possibility would be custody for one parent with unlimited visitation for the other. Both options make it clear that the children are still the responsibility of both parents. Neither parent has total control. Both must work out, incident by incident, what is best for the children. This is a painful process, but in the end it can serve the deepest needs of the children and encourage more responsible parenting.

Most of the time we were able to work out what was best for the girls. We never asked them to choose. That would have been like saying, "Who do you love the most?" and no child should *ever* be put in that position. We made the decision, and as a result, during their pre-college years the girls spent almost equal time living with their father and with me.

* * *

In a divorce proceeding, these decisions are seldom easy. They shouldn't be. You're deciding the future of living human beings—your own flesh and blood. Settling these issues is unquestionably the most difficult part of the process. If you can operate on the understanding that both parents really do love the children, you can make those decisions that will do the most to assure each child that he or she is loved in spite of the divorce. Leave them that legacy, regardless of what it may cost.

CHAPTER 13

Reacting to Divorce: Four Stages

There isn't any way to soften the word "divorce" or make it sound nice. Millions of Americans live with its reality, and for most it is a wrenching, bitter experience.

Most divorced people go through four stages in the process of coping with this reality. Each phase is important and normal—so long as you don't stay there, locked forever into seeing yourself primarily as someone's ex-mate.

1. Trauma

Despite what people may say, very few look forward to a divorce. If you initiated the action, the decision was probably painful and unnerving. If your mate initiated the divorce, most likely you sensed the news before it came, and the thought was unsettling.

In such times it is normal to respond by engaging in excessive, compulsive activity or by becoming detached from the rest of the world. This is very similar to the way most people respond to the death of loved ones.

One person shifts into a neutral emotional state. He or

she simply cannot face the world. A woman leaves her hair undone, seldom gets out of the old bathrobe, lets her housework go.

Some people will even sit alone in the dark, trying desperately to shut out any intrusion from the world outside, hoping also to shut out the painful reality of the divorce.

Another type of person can't stand to be alone. That person handles the trauma stage by becoming involved everywhere and in everything. Because the marriage relationship is breaking up, he or she fills life with every possible superficial relationship.

For both types of people, making decisions seems impossible.

Should I go to the drugstore before the grocery, or after the grocery? Should I get my hair done or not? Should I buy nonfat milk or whole milk?"

All of these little decisions become monumental, and the pain and reality are buried under a flurry of indecision. All of a person's energies are going into unimportant things in a effort to avoid dealing with the one important thing that must be faced—divorce.

STOP.

Trauma can neither be avoided nor buried in a sea of busyness.

Here's where a counselor or a trusted listener is of tremendous importance.

You've got to talk to someone—someone who won't judge you, but someone who cares enough to be tough enough to tell you when you're missing the mark or wallowing in self-pity.

There's only one way to deal with all the indecision, and that's a frontal attack. When you think of something that has to be done, write it down. Keep a list and keep it handy. Then take the most important thing, the most pressing thing on the list . . . and do that *now*.

Be good to yourself. Take yourself seriously. Don't let things slip. The longer you let them go, the less important they will seem to be. When you find yourself saying, "Well, it wasn't really *that* important," at least give that need a second look. Is it really unimportant or is it simply difficult to think about or difficult to do? Chances are that it's the latter.

This compulsive activity or self-induced neutrality can continue even after the decision to divorce is actually made. Your whole being is developing a padding between you and the reality of what is actually happening.

But you cannot avoid the raw realities of life forever. Somehow, the fact of divorce will break through your protective padding, and, at the deepest level of your being, the truth will hit with a soul-wrenching jolt. You will be thrown into . . .

2. Turmoil

You'll know when you've reached this second stage. Your response may be rage, anger, deep depression, guilt, hostility, fear, and/or anxiety. For no apparent reason, a woman may be overcome by uncontrolled crying. Or her response to divorce may be an excessive use of alcohol, tranquilizers, or heavier-than-usual smoking. A man often will suppress his feelings by burying himself in his work, by heavy drinking, or by a quick affair meant to "prove" he is still manly.

Stage two is essential in coping with divorce and in

moving toward the healing process. It may last a few weeks or a few months. Occasionally I meet a woman who shows all the signs of being in the turmoil stage, and I find she has been divorced for *fifteen years*.

The truth is that to a large extent *you* control the length of the turmoil. You can choose to make turmoil your life-style, or you may choose to experience it, and then put it behind you. Here are some suggestions.

Learn to Identify and Walk Through Your Emotions

Grieve over your sense of loss; be angry; allow yourself to feel the reality of depression and the surging feelings of hostility. Those emotions are not wrong; they are legitimate reactions to what is happening in your life. Above all, don't be caught by the idea that such emotions are sinful. As physical pain tells you something is wrong physically, so your emotions serve as signals that something is happening emotionally—something good or something bad. Learning to listen to your feelings can be your first step out of turmoil. If you are a child of God, you have the authority to bring your *feelings* under the reign of Christ as well, so that while they are fully experienced they are not out of His control.

In the midst of a heated telephone discussion with Allen, just as I was about to respond in anger, I stopped short. The realization came that I did not have to respond *instantly* to his statement. What I needed was time to think. So I simply said, "I've got to have a moment to think about what I'm feeling." Very quickly I realized I was feeling embarrassment over something, and, as a defense, I was waging a verbal battle with Allen.

That realization was a new experience for me—one of

many. That day I started taking the time to discover what I was feeling. Often, being able to label the feeling permitted me to deal with it in a more constructive, rational way.

It's *not* a case of counting to ten before you blow your top. It *is*, with the help of the Holy Spirit, sometimes calling a halt in the middle of a conversation and taking a deep breath while you sort through your feelings. What you discover about your feelings will help you understand a situation more clearly, or help you understand what you expect from people or situations.

Identifying feelings takes practice. This list will help you label your spontaneous responses to a given situation, especially in the turmoil stage.

rejection
confidence
calmness
uneasiness
gladness
grief
discomfort
joy
relaxation
elation
daring
uncertainty
boredom
pleasure
excitement
weariness
solemnity
apprehension

embarrassment
silliness
loneliness
playfulness
sadness
admiration
contentment
jealousy
caution
anger
fear
comfort
eagerness
pride
hope
childishness
discontentment

Depression is a perfectly normal response to stress and turmoil, and it will most likely visit you now and then during stage two. Don't try to do away with depression. Do attempt to identify and deal with the thing that is *causing* your depression. When you can eliminate the stressful situation or at least bring it under some measure of control, you will reduce the depression. Learn to walk through these valleys in communion with Christ, and face the fact that you will probably not eliminate all the depression. This is a tough time in your life, and it's natural to be depressed.

It's important, too, to realize that most people withdraw during the turmoil phase. They don't feel attractive. On the contrary, they feel rejected and unattractive, and this leads to withdrawal. A recently divorced person simply does not have much spare emotional energy. What little there is has to be spent coping with survival in this new world.

List Your Responsibilities

Making a list of the things I have to do (I call it a "To-Do List") gives me a feeling that I'm beginning to get a handle on things. Don't be afraid of long lists. Perhaps you should make several lists, such as, "Things I've always meant to do but haven't done," or "Things I can't settle right now," or "Things I can do to simplify my life." Writing it down isn't the same as doing it, but it's a big start. It will help to eliminate the useless, disorganized behavior that characterizes many divorced women who have told themselves they "just can't cope."

If you have things on your list that seem overwhelming right now (and you will), try to break those major tasks down into smaller tasks. Find some small thing that will start you on the road to the big task, and then *do* it.

It is often difficult for women to make decisions *on their own.* They have been conditioned to expect men to make decisions. Face that fact, and *learn to decide,* even if sometimes the decision is the wrong one.

Your overwhelming task might be to find a job—and that *is* overwhelming, especially when you are going back to work after several years. Your starting task might be "get a paper tomorrow morning and review the help-wanted ads" or "call employment agencies and set up appointments." This "To-Do List" can also double as an itemized record for your prayer agenda.

Don't saddle yourself with "Dick always told me I was a poor housekeeper. I've got to clean this old house up." Try cleaning one closet, and throwing out or giving away all the things you haven't worn in a year. Or clean out a kitchen drawer that has been filled with junk for years. Finishing tasks like these can give you a great emotional boost just when you need it most.

What you're doing here, of course, is trying to get control of a life that seems to have taken a nose dive.

Learn to tackle one thing at a time. And when it's done, give yourself the luxurious feeling of crossing it off the list. Incidentally, if your list looks too overwhelming, you may have given yourself impossible tasks. Look for the things you know you cannot do and cross them off the list. Ask yourself, "What will happen if I don't do that?" If your answer is, "Nothing," then cross it off the list.

Keeping lists will help you *see* that you are gaining control of your life, and this should help give you the strength to resist some of the "excess" advice you will begin to get from all sides. One more thing about lists and priorities: They're yours, so don't be afraid to change them when you need to.

Learn to Be Creative With Your Solitude

Your whole world has been two-by-two. But now it has changed, and the natural tendency is to do everything possible to avoid being alone. A woman with children will become super-involved with them and her house until she falls asleep early from utter exhaustion. A man will go here, there, and anywhere until he comes home and drops into bed.

An alternative is to try to see the pleasure of solitude. Attempt to cherish the quietness. Make it a time of prayerful meditation and conversation with your heavenly Comforter. Discover that this time can provide you with spiritual and emotional renewal. Keep a daily journal, using it to record your most private thoughts and dreams.

At this stage, nothing can take away the loneliness. But you can make the solitude a friend rather than an enemy.

For a divorced person, nothing seems such a stark reminder of the change in his or her life as the *empty bed.*

My response was to do something feminine to the bed, just to make it *mine*. I bought satin sheets and pillowcases that I couldn't afford. But they gave me a feeling of real luxury—a *new* feeling. Then I began sleeping in the middle of the bed.

On Saturday mornings I fixed myself breakfast, and ate it in bed. It helped.

Some men have told me that they put the bed away or even gave it away. In its place they used a sleeping bag—on the floor. That was their new sleeping experience, one that also provided them with a feeling of intimacy.

With regard to *meals*, if you have children, the tendency often is to eat quick convenience foods or take the kids out to the local hamburger stand. "I just can't stand to cook anymore" is the excuse. As a start, why not help the children plan the meals and let them cook? Or force yourself to try some new dish you've always wanted to prepare.

If you're alone, an "empty" table (one without your mate) is difficult. And you'll probably avoid it as long as you can. But eating out isn't all that easy either. Restaurants don't seem to know what to do with singles, unless you sit at the counter. Hostesses left me waiting or seated me by the kitchen door until I learned to ask for a better table. Recently a hostess asked, "Are you alone?" And I responded, "No, there are forty-seven million of us."

Snacking all night or going without doesn't work for long, and you probably can't afford to eat out every night. At this stage, you're probably not ready to invite someone for dinner. So eventually you're going to have to fix your own dinner—and eat it alone. But treat yourself well. Fix something you really like. Get out the good china and tableware. If you don't have a crystal goblet, buy one. Remove the extra chairs from the table. Make the difficult meal as much of an event as you can.

Boldly Ask for Help When You Need It

Car Repairs, for example, usually are no problem for men, but they represent a whole new world for most women. Ask some man you know—a neighbor, friend, or relative—whom he trusts, and try that mechanic. When your car needs repairs, ask for a detailed estimate in advance. Ask questions. Unless your car won't move another inch, don't be afraid to get another mechanic's opinion.

If you regularly buy your gas at a self-service station, go to a full-service station at least once a month so they can check your oil and water. Those important things are easily forgotten.

Money will probably be a difficult problem, especially if you have children. It is estimated that it now costs $70,000 to raise a child from the cradle through college. That's difficult for most families and monumental for most single parents. The salary of the average working mother minus babysitting expenses is going to make strict budgeting necessary. You are going to need all the help you can get.

I knew almost nothing about money when I was divorced, and the learning process has been painfully slow.

In the weeks immediately following the divorce, especially watch your financial commitments. Life is pretty shaky; don't make it worse by over-obligating yourself.

Talk to your banker. If you don't have one, get one. The officers in a small branch always seem to me to have more time for questions. Tell the banker your story—not all the details, but enough to help him understand your financial concerns and questions.

When things aren't working out as you planned, go back to "your banker." Usually he'll do whatever he can to help. To this day I have a terrible time balancing my checkbook. About once a quarter I take all my canceled checks and statements in to my banker, and together we straighten out the mess. Banks are willing to help.

Don't Be Afraid to Fail

Suggestions can so easily sound like rules. And right now, failure of any kind can add to the already heavy load of guilt and pain.

Relax. You're probably going to fail *somewhere* in the recovery process. But don't be alarmed. Don't despair. When Peter (who had failed to the extent of denying the Lord) asked Jesus about forgiveness, he said: "'Master, if my brother goes on wronging me how often should I forgive him? Would seven times be enough?'

" 'No,' replied Jesus, 'not seven times, but seventy times seven!'" (Matt. 18:21,22, *Phillips).*

Don't let the fear of failure keep you from acting. If you play safe, you'll never accomplish anything.

One sure sign that you are moving out of the turmoil stage is that you have made yourself seek out new relationships. You're probably not dating, but you have decided that the time has come to rejoin the world. You want to be with others. That's the mark of the next stage . . .

Adjustment

Now you are beginning to explore the possibility that life can go on. You're discovering a new world. Your mind is less and less filled with thoughts of your ex-mate. He or she is not gone from your mind completely, but there is room now for other, more productive thoughts.

You can begin to move off self-center and begin to think caringly about other people. Your compulsive need to tell all of the painful details of your divorce to anyone who will listen has decreased. You can actually begin to hear someone else's pain, maybe even listen sympathetically to *their* "divorce story."

You are ready to enjoy more fully the new things you began so tentatively in the turmoil stage. New interests have begun to develop; follow them now in greater depth. You can feel free to drop the classes that are not holding your interest. You gave them the old college try, but now you know that it isn't what you want to do. You're free to change, to decide what is good and life-supporting for you.

Perhaps most of all, your focus has begun to change. Your concentration is less and less on what you *used* to be. The recovery steps you took in the turmoil stage are taking root. You *are* becoming a new person. Life *is* starting again.

When you begin to feel those signs of new life, the next steps are simply a repeat of what you have already been doing. But now you can do them more aggressively, more freely.

Remind yourself of the progress you are making. It may not be evident in a comparison of one day with the next. But look back a week or two, or a month. That's where you'll see the progress. Thank God for His help, and don't forget to congratulate yourself on the progress. You might treat yourself to a very nice dinner, knowing that, to the extent that God is a vital part of your life, He will be your unseen but very welcome Guest.

Celebrate every bit of progress in your own special way. But however you do it, be very sure to take note of the fact that things *have* changed.

Something else is changing, too. Something deep inside, in your attitude toward life. The pain has not vanished but there will be times when you can feel real joy *through* the pain.

The great Christian statesman, E. Stanley Jones, tells us that "during the Madagascar persecutions, groups gathered in caves and holes to worship. Such a group, bursting with love and gratitude, said to their leader, 'Let us sing.'

"'Brethren, I implore you to keep quiet,' said their leader. 'Our enemies are looking for us, and it will be death to all of us if we are caught.'

"'But we must sing,' they said in a low voice.

"So, under their breaths, these Christians sang."

Adjustment does not mean that the tears and the turmoil are over . . . forever. They may return without warning. But the process has begun. New life is beginning. We have hope to hold onto. And soon adjustment gives way to . . .

Reconstruction

Line upon line, brick by brick, you can now build a new life. The journey is unpredictable. There will be crises along the way. But God who makes new persons from broken lives is present in love to help us pick up the pieces and experience the miracle of recovery.

Continue to stay with the things that prodded you into growth. Keep at the things that are life producing. Remember that growth is not one-dimensional. The truly whole person grows emotionally, spiritually, physically, and intellectually.

Cultivate a healthy curiosity. Explore something new as often as you can. Look up a new word in the dictionary. Begin a book you've always wanted to read. Get growing.

Cherish simple things: a beautiful cloud bank, a star-filled sky, the unbelievable detail of a wild flower, the beautiful perfume of the out-of-doors after a rain.

Encourage new relationships and keep old caring relationships alive. Sharpen your listening skills, so that you can learn to enjoy people more fully. Strive to spend quality time with the people you really care about, time to talk about things. Feel the freedom to share insignificant things, but make time to share the deep things—things you don't share with "just anyone." Find simple, thoughtful ways to say "thank you" for a kindness. Even a postcard will show you care and appreciate a friend. Why not carry a few with you in a pocket or purse?

Let prayer and inner quietness enrich your life. Find a book that can help you learn how to pray and respond to God more fully. Make a daily appointment with God and keep it. Think on the love and power of God.

Spend times in a caring fellowship that will help to support you spiritually. Sometimes a large church with its full program may feel unfriendly to a divorced person. But don't give up easily. Often you will find another searcher, and together you can look for the small caring fellowship in the church.

Learn to enjoy the worship service of the church. One sure way to keep your life in perspective is to regularly stop to appreciate the grandeur and greatness of God, and to remind yourself that you are of special concern to this great God.

Allow yourself to feel the security of God's love. There is something very solid, very life-supporting in the realization that you are loved by God, even though you are known totally by Him.

Relax. You are loved.

CHAPTER 14

Getting to Know Yourself Again

It generally takes from two to three years to significantly recover from a divorce.

That may be the most painful statistic you will ever face. I can almost hear the groaning. For most, the intensity of the turmoil stage itself doesn't last that long. But generally it *does* take that long for a comfortable, whole person to emerge.

As I said, once not long ago you were two. Now you are one. And that will take some getting used to. There's an empty place in your life. It's natural to think of yourself as two; you did for so long.

In a recent television drama, a widow was going out on a date, and the idea was very uncomfortable to her. "I can't date," she protested. "I'm a married woman."

"Momma," her daughter broke in, "Daddy's been gone for *fifteen years.*"

Don't live in the old identity. It's a waste of effort to concentrate on what *was*. Like it or not, that is over. The absence of a mate certainly creates a void in your life. But don't make the void larger than it really is by making it the center of your focus.

It is a perfectly natural tendency to want to fill the void

with something . . . anything. Some fill it with activity. Some fill it with people. In the beginning, they simply want to be around people, lots of people. Then, out of the crowd, they find one warm body that shows interest. Life feels like it's falling into place again. The waves have calmed, and that awful loneliness is slipping away.

Now the tendency is to act out the old drama once more in a new, more exciting relationship. And you can almost be assured of what is going to happen because, perhaps unconsciously, you have *repeated* the old relationship.

Wait just a minute. All this concentration on filling the void with someone is keeping you from the very things that will bring you the deepest, richest recovery from divorce.

I understand the need to fill up the emptiness—oh, how *well* I understand it! But I urge you to give yourself some breathing room. One significant relationship has just broken up. No matter how badly you were treated by your mate, you were a part of the union. You were either a contributor to the break, or you have been scarred by it in some way—most likely, both.

Give yourself time for healing. Now that your life is no longer entwined with another's, take this time to discover who you really are. In big and small ways you have been performing for someone. Probably you have even been dressing to conform to someone else's tastes. Because you were two, you gave up little pieces of your identity, and while you were two that was good. But that era of your life has ended.

It's time to take a deep breath and start the recovery process—that is, if you *really* want to recover.

The Gospel of John records a most unusual story about Jesus' encounter with a sick man who has been at a pool called Bethzatha for thirty-eight years. He and other sick people surrounded the pool daily, waiting for the water to be moved by an angel. If an angel touched the water, the first person who slipped into the water would be healed.

"When Jesus saw him lying there on his back—knowing that he had been like that for a long time—he said to him, 'Do you want to get well again?' " (John 5:6, *Phillips*).

What an amazing question for Jesus to ask a man who had been ill for thirty-eight years! But Jesus knew the human personality well enough to know that no matter what the sickness or how serious the pain, there is something strangely secure in a life that has narrowed down to regularity and routine, even if the routine centers on pain and disability. Sometimes we hold on to the known pain rather than trade it for the uncertainty of the open road. The path to recovery has lots of question marks. Knowing that, Jesus asked, "Do you *want* to get well again?"

Even though the healing process will be costly, you have an exhilarating world of new freedoms to gain. Increasingly, you will discover what it means to be free from. . .

. . . being trapped by your emotions
. . . being controlled and manipulated by other people
. . . the fear of failure
. . . the need for self-pity
. . . the frustration of not knowing who you are
. . . the insecurity of not knowing where you are going.

If you're ready for the journey, let's take a deep breath and get started. We've got lots of discovering to do.

When the process started for me—just after my first divorce—I had no idea who I was or what I liked. I didn't know how to buy clothing for myself. I didn't know whether I really liked the foods I had eaten for years or whether I liked them because the rest of my family did.

Now, for the first time in years, I could shop for *me*. Walking up and down the aisles of the supermarket was an adventure. When I saw something that attracted me I'd ask myself, "Do I really like that?" I'd think about the question and then buy what I thought I would *really* like.

I did the same thing with clothing. Instead of buying what George would like (George was my current date) I dressed to maximize myself. I stopped looking for particular brands of clothes. And I learned not to be influenced by salesclerks. To their insistent offers of help I now respond, "I'm just looking. I really don't know what I want. But I'll let you know when I want to try something on." I have found this to be one small way to practice being more assertive, and it has given me the freedom to decide on clothing for myself.

And the process goes on and on. Even today, I'm still discovering what I really like. I still ask myself, "Why am I doing this? Why am I buying this? What type of music do I want to listen to? Is this furniture the kind I really like?"

To my surprise, I found that I love old buildings with lots of wood, and antique furniture, and classical music. I had thought before that glass and chrome and modern things were right for me. Now I'm more comfortable with my surroundings, and with myself.

This is also the time to begin to find out what your interests are. Taking classes is a great way to find out whether or not you really like a particular thing. It doesn't cost much to explore an interest. Check a local community college; you'll find an amazing collection of classes.

The class routine will get you out of the house, especially if you have to pay a little for the class. You'll be exploring something new, and you'll be meeting other people with the same interest.

If you find you don't like that thing after all, drop the class. Don't lock yourself into something distasteful. But if you like it, stay with it. You've discovered another piece of who you are.

Include some physical activity in this discovery process. Now that you've gotten up from your chair in front of the TV, it's time to take good care of yourself. And again, try various things until you find the thing you really like.

If you're trying something new, don't be afraid to ask for help. Most people enjoy helping a beginner. Sometimes a new activity is frightening. If I sense that I am scared to try something, I tell my friends I'm going to do that thing on a particular weekend. I know that on Monday they're going to ask how things went, and that seems to give me the extra push I need.

What Do I Value?

There's another way to get a good look at yourself.

Do your best to rank the values in Figure A in the order of their true importance to you. Remember, no one is looking over your shoulder. There's nobody to impress. As you put the values in the order of their importance to you, try to think of specific situations where those values were involved. This will help you to rank the values as you *really* see them.

Try not to group values ("Health, emotional well-being, and honesty are all number 1 for me"). This defeats the value of the exercise. As you get new insights, don't hesitate to use the eraser and change the order of your values.

Figure A

___	Justice	The quality of being impartial or fair, righteousness; conformity to truth, fact, or reason; treating others fairly or adequately.
___	Altruism	Regard for or devotion to the interests of others.
___	Recognition	Being made to feel significant and important; being given special notice or attention.
___	Pleasure	The agreeable emotion accompanying the possession or expectation of what is good or greatly desired. "Pleasure" stresses satisfaction or gratification rather than visible happiness; a state of gratification.
___	Wisdom	The ability to discern inner qualities and relationships; insight, good sense, judgment.
___	Achievement	Accomplishment; a result brought about by resolve, persistence, or endeavor. The word "achieve" is defined as "to bring to a successful conclusion; to accomplish; to attain a desired end or aim."
___	Honesty	Fairness or straightforwardness of conduct; integrity; uprightness of character or action.

___	Autonomy	The ability to be a self-determining individual.
___	Wealth	Abundance of valuable material possessions or resources; affluence.
___	Power	Possession of control, authority, or influence over others.
___	Love	Affection based on admiration or benevolence; warm attachment, enthusiasm, or devotion; unselfish devotion that freely accepts another in loyalty and seeks his good.
___	Aesthetics	The appreciation and enjoyment of beauty for beauty's sake.
___	Physical Appearance	Concern for the beauty of one's body.
___	Health	The condition of being sound in body; freedom from physical disease or pain; the general condition of the body; well-being.
___	Skill	The ability to use one's knowledge effectively and readily in execution or performance; technical expertise.
___	Emotional Well-Being	Freedom from overwhelming anxieties and barriers to effective functioning; peace of mind; inner security.
___	Knowledge	The seeking of truth, information, or principles for the satisfaction of curiosity, for use, or for the power of knowing.
___	Morality	The belief in and keeping of ethical standards.

____	Faith in God	Communion with, obedience to, and activity in behalf of the Lord Jesus Christ.
____	Loyalty	Maintaining allegiance to a person, group or institution, or political entity.

Success Experiences

Past experiences in which you felt successful can give you clues to who you are. Even though life may be dark right now, you *have* had success experiences.

On a piece of paper (see Figure B), divide your life into three periods: for example, birth–16, 17–25, 26–present. Choose any divisions you want.

In each time period, list five success experiences. Be careful that you don't look for world-changing kinds of successes. A success experience might be when the teacher put your artwork on display in the first grade.

Don't be afraid to take your time. Enjoy the trip into your memory. As you remember something, write it down in a phrase or a sentence.

In the second column, describe in a few words why you felt successful.

Now look for some insights. On this paper are some of the things that have made you feel good about yourself. As you begin to enjoy this new discovery, use the insights you have gained to complete the sentence, "I feel successful when . . ."

Figure B

Success Experiences	Why I felt Successful

I feel successful when . . .

This little exercise can give you a completely new picture of yourself, and you will get new ideas to pursue in the months ahead.

Everybody wants a fulfilled life. For me, the fulfilled life is made up of

- balance
- maturity
- serenity
- joy
- caring
- sensitivity
- humor
- accomplishment
- acceptance
- love

It would be helpful for you to define each of these words from your present perspective. What do they mean *to you*? Then rearrange the words by numbering them in order of their importance to you in your search for fulfillment.

Each of these elements is essential for a fulfilled life. Make special note of those qualities you feel you need to develop.

Dreaming Dreams

At a time when life seems to be simply a matter of survival, it doesn't seem to make sense to dream. But, in fact, there will never be a better time. Your life is taking a new direction, so give yourself the luxury of looking at your future.

Consider this question: If you could do anything you wanted, if you knew you could not fail, and if you had all the money, resources, and talent that you needed, what would you be doing one year from now? What would you be doing five years from now?

Of course, you will always have limitations. Everyone does. But every once in a while it's good to ignore the limitations and look squarely at what you'd really like to do. Who knows, you *might* want to try in spite of limitations. Or maybe you can decide on a first step and try that.

Make some more lists. The more you learn about what you want to do, the more you can break those big things down into smaller, more manageable, more readily accomplished tasks. Do those, one at a time. Start becoming the person you were meant to be.

When you have a real choice, don't take on things you

don't want to do. Be careful about making commitments. Take the time to find out how important something is to people you care about, and to you, before you agree to do it. Once you agree to do something, make every effort to fulfill your commitment.

Remove as much of the clutter from your life as possible—cluttered drawers and closets, for sure (I got rid of two-thirds of my wardrobe when I did this). And cluttered schedules. Again, it's back to lists. Make a daily "to-do" list and begin to organize your day. You'll save time, travel, and maybe even money.

Relationships

The more relationships you feel compelled to cut, the more acute will be your sense of loss. Maintain every relationship you can that is important or rewarding to you. If you *can* continue in some club or group, by all means do so. It will give you a feeling of continuity that can be very helpful. So much will be new that it will be good to have some ties to the past.

As a first step toward developing new relationships, try taking a personal interest in the people around you. Let them know you care. This isn't being nosy; it's just showing an interest and listening more. Remember the concerns they talk about and ask how things are going. Don't push. They'll know if you're really interested, and you'll be surprised how many people will respond.

The Church

Avoid spiritual isolation. Even though a church may not be all you might hope for at this time in your life, it *is* a supportive family. Somewhere in the church are the five percent who will really care about you and understand. Look for them. They are worth the search and the struggle.

Divorce often will drive you either to God *or* away from Him. The direction *you* go is not God's fault—nor the church's, for that matter. Like so much in this new life, the responsibility rests squarely on your shoulders.

I found a relationship with God to be a forgiving, loving, supportive relationship. For me He was "a friend who sticks closer than a brother" (Prov. 18:24, NASB).

Attitudes

Since my attitudes seem to cover the entire spectrum, leaping without warning from contentment to negativism, how do I bring them under control? Where do I find normalcy?

The first step is to determine that your ex-mate is not going to define or shape your disposition. What he or she does is *none of your business.*

"But . . ." I can hear millions protesting (well, maybe not millions, but at least thousands), "Do you know what that __________ did to me?"

As long as you allow yourself to react in that fashion, your ex-mate is very much in control. How *you* react is *your* business. You *can* control *that*.

In the period immediately following a crisis, I believe it is healthy to get your anger out in a way that will do no damage to your ex-mate. In the presence of a counselor or a trusted, unshockable friend, say what you're really feeling. The process is something like the lancing of a boil. You won't like the foul stuff that bursts out, but getting it out is far better than allowing it to poison your entire system.

Anger in and of itself is not sinful or destructive. But when you allow it to smolder—thinking about it, nurturing it, and keeping it alive—*that* is sinful and destructive. The entire process of growth is brought to a screeching halt.

Get the anger out of your system and get on with the process of living.

Once you have dealt with the rage, remember the reflecting method we talked about earlier. When your stomach muscles begin to tighten, the pressure rises, and your adrenalin starts flowing, STOP. Say to yourself, "What am I feeling? Am I angry . . . anxious . . . what is it?"

Be sure you hear what is being said. Think about what you heard. Deal with any feelings and *then* respond. For how you respond can make a big difference in communication. "You" messages destroy communication and make the other party defensive. "You didn't pay the child support on time, and I got such a stomach ache I had to take a day off from work."

Contrast this with the very same information expressed as an "I" message. "I became very tense worrying about our finances this month when I didn't get the child support check." One message accuses; the other simply reports a difficult situation. One says what "you" did; the other tells the same story in terms of how "I" felt. "I" messages take practice, but they save a lot of ex-mate squabbles. It works with the children, too. Try it.

Finding a Confidant

If you have any friends at all, you will have a tendency to tell *all* to *everybody*. You may feel that any listening ear needs to get the whole story of what a skunk your ex-mate was. Pretty soon, friends tire of hearing that old song. The first time they were supportive. Now they want to leave and go to the next room or, if possible, the next county.

You're caught in a cycle. First it's "I hate him," then "I love him." Then it's "I love him. I want him back." Without a moment's notice, you slip back to "I hate him. I want to get him." That cycle of feelings is very real to you, but to a friend it sounds as if you're losing your mind. If your friend points out your inconsistencies, you're embarrassed, and the friendship is strained.

Both men *and* women face this "feeling cycle." Men say to me, "I can't make up my mind what to do. Sometimes she drives me nuts. Other times I go to see her expecting a big fight, and she turns me on so much. All I want to do is take her in my arms and say, 'Come on, honey, let's put this thing back together again.' But I know better. I know it won't work."

Those feelings are normal. But the whole world is not

waiting to hear them. You need *one* trusted confidant, someone who will listen without making judgments. For me, that person was a professional counselor. You may have a friend who can fill that role. If that person is a non-professional, let him know you want to use him as a dumping ground and get his approval. Explain that, especially at first, you don't want a garbage *inspector*. You don't need to be analyzed. You just need a person who will listen to your anger and frustration.

It is good if that person can support you in prayer. Ultimately, as your emotional wounds begin to heal, your confidant can offer you some feedback, helping you to see what you are saying.

Will Singleness Ever Feel Good?

As time and your emotional growth separate you from your ex-mate, and you feel less like half of a former twosome and more like a whole person, you're ready to think of singleness as a gift.

I can tell you that it is a gift—and tell you, and tell you, and tell you some more. But that can never make it a gift for you. Our culture makes most people more comfortable as part of a couple. Only you can tell yourself that this single state is a gift.

Well, you and the apostle Paul: "I wish that all men were like myself, but I realize that everyone has his own particular *gift* from God" (1 Cor. 7:7, *Phillips*, italics mine).

Singleness is not *better* than marriage. Both are gifts.

In order to test Jesus, the Pharisees asked Him

whether or not it was right for a man to divorce his wife on any grounds whatever. Jesus explained that the divorce law was altered because of the wickedness of man's heart and the brokenness of his relationships. But, He explained, it was never God's intention for it to be that way.

Then He went on to say that "anyone who divorces his wife on any grounds except her unfaithfulness, and marries some other woman, commits adultery."

This was some strong medicine. The disciples responded with something like, "Well, if that's the way it is then it's better not to get married in the first place!"

"'It is not everybody who can live up to this,' replied Jesus,'—only those who have a special gift'" (Matt. 19:11, *Phillips)*.

There it is again. Singleness is a gift. For me that realization opened up a whole new world. I didn't take a vow of celibacy. I didn't stop dating. I didn't stop enjoying the company of men. But a quiet contentment began to work its way into my busy life. I was able to stop pursuing marriage and to begin my pursuit of life. I was able to live less and less in some rosy, hoped-for future and to begin living in the *now*.

Thoughts About Being "In Love"

Falling in love is one of the hazards of the divorced person. If you read the first part of this book, you know I speak from experience.

Somewhere in my process of falling in and out of love, I discovered that the person who is always mooning and crooning over someone—always "in love"—is an insecure, unstable person. We recognize that symptom in young people, but we excuse the same thing in ourselves.

Psychologists say that the average person falls in love six or seven times before marriage and another six or seven times *after* marriage.

In a two-year study, Dr. Anthony Campolo discovered that "love" is what you are in now. "Infatuation" was what you felt with the person you broke up with.

A counselor tells of men reporting to him, "I'm in love with my secretary." His response, tempered by years of experience, is, "Wait two months. It will probably go away." Generally it does.

Don't get me wrong. Romance is lovely. The candlelight, the flowers, and all the extra courtesies are exciting. They make you feel attractive at a time when you most need reinforcement.

But don't expect those feelings to last. Don't fall for the line that says being in love is the ultimate emotional fulfillment. Take your time. Find out if this person is really good for you. Are you good for him or for her?

The more mature you become, the more recovery you allow. You'll become a more attractive person. You'll make more of your own choices. The recovery process will begin to feel exciting and fulfilling.

You're on your way to becoming the person God intended you to be.

Enjoy the sunrise. It's yours.

CHAPTER 15

Forgiveness Is a Process

"Don't talk to *me* about forgiveness." I hear that all the time from divorced people. "*He* (or *she*) is the one who needs forgiveness."

No single subject raises so much complaint or objection among divorced people. Yet nothing poisons the human personality and retards emotional growth and recovery like unforgiveness.

Raise the subject of forgiveness, and immediately I am reminded of all the painful things my mate put me through. Sometimes I can't remember my own telephone number, but I can remember specific details of those long-ago hurts. To protect myself and justify my own actions, I've kept detailed accounts in my memory bank. Many times when it didn't seem that I could go one step further or even make it through some crisis with the kids, remembering how badly I was treated gave me the will to keep on going.

"Forgive my mate? *No way*!"

But some principles are so basic to life that you cannot escape their power. Their insistent message cannot be drowned out, no matter how hard you try.

Many years ago Jesus said, "For if you forgive other people their failures, your Heavenly Father will also forgive you. But if you will not forgive other people, neither will your Heavenly Father forgive you your failures" (Matt. 6:14,15, *Phillips).*

"O.K.! O.K.! I'll *try* to forgive." Perhaps you try—again and again. But the sour feeling is still there in the pit of your stomach. Some old memory comes flooding back, or some new event reminds you of the bitter past . . . and the old anger is back again.

"I thought I'd forgiven him (or her). Won't this thing ever end?"

At this point it's easy to conclude that you just *can't* forgive. You know you need to. The idea sounds right. But it just doesn't work, at least for you.

Before very long you're again facing the need to forgive. It *is* one of those things that just won't go away. But this time your response is different. You tried to forgive—tried very hard, in fact. And it didn't work. So now instead of trying again, you feel guilty. "Why can't I forgive? It must be that I'm a bad person."

"No," you tell yourself. "Look what he (or she) did to me." And once again you go over the details, sometimes reciting them for others, trying to justify your inability to forgive. "It must be that he (or she) hurt me so deeply. That's it. That's the reason I can't forgive."

And the vicious circle goes on and on, holding you in its dark grasp: remember—forgive—I can't—guilt—justify myself—remember . . .

Who Wronged Whom?

In a marriage, hurt is almost always a two-way street. Each mate has done his or her share of the hurting. This simply means that I cannot honestly look back on our relationship without recognizing my own need for forgiveness.

The place to start is at home, with yourself. First, ask God for forgiveness.

"If we confess our sins, He is faithful and righteous to forgive us our sins and to cleanse us from all unrighteousness" (1 John 1:9, NASB).

Very early in life we learn that we must never admit to being wrong. How foolish! And how destructive to loving, open, honest relationships. This inability to admit wrong breeds distrust and antagonism. It hurts us all. How do we learn to admit guilt, to ask for forgiveness?

1. By understanding the need for it.
2. By learning that admitting we are wrong does not show weakness, but *strength*.
3. By practicing it on little things every hour of every day, and thus learning to take care of the big goofs.
4. By learning to be completely honest with ourselves about those times when we are wrong.

It is so important to the whole process for us to ask forgiveness of those we have wronged. Such simple words: "I was wrong. I'm sorry. Please forgive me." They are said so seldom, but what miracles of healing and restoration they bring about.

No one knows how to con me better than I do. If I begin to sense that I'm wrong about something, I am very good at arguing my own case, "proving" to myself that I'm right. In the midst of this, I've had to learn to stop everything and face what is happening. If I can *right then* say, "You're right. I'm wrong. I'm sorry," it's less painful than if I wait. Time and guilt will make me more defensive than ever.

But what about the ones who will not forgive us, or those who are not around for us to ask forgiveness of?

Learn to forgive, for your own sake. A lack of forgiveness will seldom harm the other person; it only breeds hostility in you. You can go through life drinking a glass of bitterness every morning and spewing it out on the world the rest of the day, if that's the way you want to live. But I'll tell you this: It's *your* stomach that will suffer, your life that will be damaged by the poison.

None of us—I mean NONE of us—has been *so wronged* that we are not commanded to forgive. Have you been more wronged than Jesus Christ? He prayed for the forgiveness of his enemies. Cast into a German concentration camp because she protected Jews, Corrie ten Boom was able, years later, to forgive the German guard who tortured her and was most responsible for her sister's death.

Easy? Hardly. Read her account of it in *The Hiding Place*. She was dumbfounded at the very idea that she should forgive that guard. But she did. And I'm sure that the forgiveness was much more healing for Corrie than it was for the guard.

Once we have been forgiven, we must learn to forgive ourselves. We may live with the *consequences* of our sins for a long time; there is little that can change that reality. But we can learn to forgive ourselves.

When God forgives us, He forgets our sin. "I will forgive their iniquity, and *their sin I will remember no more*" (Jer. 31:34, NASB, italics mine).

What God forgets we have no right to remember. Once we are forgiven, we can forgive ourselves and begin to allow the experience to fade from our memory.

When Karen was about six, I punished her unjustly. I didn't hurt her physically, but I could never forget the hurt in her eyes. Years later I would remember that incident with such pain of regret and feelings of guilt that I could hardly stand it. The memory of it colored my relationship with Karen. Guilt is *always* destructive. Sometimes, because of the guilt I felt, I wouldn't discipline her when she needed it. And because guilt breeds hostility, there were times when I was too harsh on her. Then the cycle would begin all over again.

I still remember that incident with shame and a little sadness. But Karen forgave me, and since I've forgiven myself it doesn't come back to haunt me.

We are assured of God's forgiveness. We can learn to forgive ourselves, and with that dual forgiveness comes the ability to forget, to the extent that, should we remember the event, the sting and the destructive anger are gone.

Forgiveness Is a Process

No one can jump the Grand Canyon in a single leap. Why, then, do we think we can forgive someone for the collective hurts of two or ten or twenty years in one giant leap? Forgiveness is a process. It needs to be achieved a step at a time.

No place in the church have I ever heard people explaining to other people, especially to divorced people, that forgiveness is a process. The church says very clearly, "You must." And this is absolutely right. But one gets the feeling that God drops forgiveness like a shroud, and then we are able to forgive. That simply isn't true.

You must come to the realization within your own heart that to forgive someone else is something God wants you to do for *yourself*, more than for the other person. Not to forgive means eventually to make yourself mentally, emotionally, and physically ill. It's always possible to forgive. If Corrie ten Boom can forgive after the great injustices she suffered, anybody can forgive anybody. I'm not saying you can do it without God's grace, but you can do it.

The question is *how*!

Very slowly.

Every time your anger rises at something that even reminds you of a hurt, you have to ferret that out and deal with it immediately. Don't lump it together with all the other things that person has done to you. Just deal with that one thing alone. Look at it and try to understand why the person did it to you. Would *you* ever do that in similar circumstances? Take a good look at it. Is it worth carrying around, knowing it will turn into hostility that makes *you* hard and angry? Probably not. Ask God for grace to forgive that. Then forgive it. And *forget it*!

If it starts to edge itself into your mind after that, throw it out! Don't indulge yourself in remembrances of it. When you're feeling sorry for yourself, you tend to resurrect forgotten wrongs. Do yourself a favor, and don't.

What a lovely thing forgiveness is—both in the getting and the giving of it. It brings peace, calmness, and a good feeling of self-worth.

It's hard work, but it's worth it!

CHAPTER 16

Relationships—Shattered But Not Scattered

"People who need people are the luckiest people in the world." The song says it, but don't believe the part about being lucky.

Some people withdraw after a divorce. Others fill their lives with every superficial relationship they can manage. The more people they are around, the more they feel as if nothing has changed.

In fact, everything has changed. Virtually all the relationships in their lives have been affected by what has happened. Everyone is concerned about a divorce. Friends and family are sincerely saddened, but they can't pick up a card at the local Hallmark card shop that says "Sorry you're divorcing." There's a card for every *other* occasion great and small, but not for this. No one quite knows how to respond when a friend or loved one is divorced.

Uncomfortable or not, divorced people *do* need others. As much as possible, life needs to go on and, in a way, life means relationships. In spite of all the awkwardness we may feel, relationships tie us to the real world and help pull us out of despair and get us back to the business of living.

The natural tendency for the divorced person who is leaving the turmoil stage and beginning to find people again is to search out other singles. You can find them in clubs and church singles' groups and Parents Without Partners—lots of places. Remember, there are millions of singles now, and more coming all the time. The singles' world is a big world and a good one. Go out and find it. More than likely you'll be readily accepted.

Enjoy that sense of belonging, that place of new identity. But remember this: Single is what has happened to you. It's your *state*. It is *not* who you are, any more than your height or the color of your eyes is who you are. Don't allow your world to be narrowed down to singles *only*. That is not the whole world, and it shouldn't be your whole world.

It's good to have *children* in your life. They bring back a touch of wonder and reality. Out of a child's skinned knees and bug collections, baseball gloves and fingernail polish, God can fashion a whole world of warmth for the icy landscape of a lonely life.

If you don't have children of your own, borrow someone else's. I do, now that my girls are grown. I met Sarah and Jana at my office (their mother works with me). We sat and talked one day when they came in. Later on I had dinner at their home, and the girls showed me their room. A few weeks later, I offered to babysit free. And that night our friendship developed.

We get together now and then, and sometimes I take them to lunch and a movie on Saturday. We have a great time. They teach me how to play and how to dream. They enrich my life and give me a sense of balance I would not have otherwise.

It took a while, but finally I decided that I also needed

married people in my life. When I began to feel better about myself—more secure as a person, no longer half of something—I was ready to have married friends. Many times as we talk they pull me into shape when my attitude is slipping back into the old "me-against-the-world" pattern. And they make it easy for me to get a male viewpoint from someone other than a date.

Married people are good for me, and I think I'm good for them. But don't stop there. You need *older people* in your life. Once again, if you don't have them, go out and find them.

Sitting alone one day at a table in a crowded coffee shop, I heard an older lady say, "Do you mind if I sit here at your table?" Surprised, I looked up and quickly recovered to say, "No. Please do."

That was my introduction to Lucille. "When you're eighty, you can do this kind of thing," she explained as she sat down. Lucille brought a touch of charm and delight to that otherwise very ordinary lunch. She told me that, for something to do, she goes to a retirement home "to visit the old folks." It turns out that one of Lucille's "old folks" is a seventy-year-old man.

As our lunch ended, it just seemed natural to ask for Lucille's phone number. She had too much to give me to just let her slip out of my life. She made me think about how I wanted to be when I got to be eighty. I met her almost four years ago, and during the years since then we've gone out to dinner at least once a month. Time and again I've said to Lucille, "You make me feel good." And she tells me she feels the same way about me. I like our relationship, and I highly recommend that you let some young senior citizen slip into your life.

There's nothing wrong with vegetating for a night or

two now and then. But ask yourself this question: "Do I want to do this the rest of my life?" Even if your answer is only a timid, tentative no, do something about it. Take some risks. Develop new relationships. Don't get caught in the narrow world of singles only.

Children

Young children tend to think of the divorce as their fault. We've already talked about helping them to understand that that isn't so.

Before long their feelings may change, and you can expect to find traces of "it is *your* fault" that Daddy (or Mommy) isn't around anymore. Encourage children to tell you what they are feeling. Even their angry feelings are okay.

Divorce is traumatic for children. Like grown-ups, they have strong feelings. But they have no way to act out those feelings. They can't divorce anybody. They can't leave anybody or start a new life. They are left with the broken pieces, powerless to do anything but live with them and bury them inside. Encourage them to express their feelings, and let them know they will not be judged or punished for doing so.

If they do express angry feelings, be prepared as best you can to respond non-defensively in patience. Whatever your children say, try not to take it personally. They are responding to their sense of loss, and their anger is normal and healthy. And *never* use what they say against them.

Show Loving Concern

I remember how, after I left Allen, Karen would complain of stomachaches. In school the pain was so bad she would be in tears. The school nurse would call to see if Karen could come home. Time after time it had happened, and time after time Allen refused to let her come home. "The doctor says there's nothing wrong with her," was Allen's response. "She's all right. Keep her in school."

When I found out what was happening, I was angry. "Karen needs to be loved and cuddled. She needs to be cared for. Someone needs to take her pain seriously," I would yell into the telephone at Allen.

I thought his response was wrong, and I knew mine was right. He was being unconcerned, calloused. Looking back now, I can see how much my response was triggered by guilt. The divorce situation was all my fault, I felt. If we had been together there wouldn't have been any stomachaches, and even if there had been, we could have talked together about our response to Karen. (I *am* sure I was right to speak up for tenderness and caring, regardless of what triggered that response.)

Those Little Manipulators

Children are masters at emotional blackmail. Divorce often seems to sharpen those skills. Over and over again I heard, "Dad doesn't let us go to those kinds of movies. Dad doesn't let us have that kind of dessert. Dad doesn't let us do this or that."

Nine times out of ten *you* don't want them to do that, either. But you're being set up. You want to be a hero in their eyes, and you certainly want them to think of Dad as a scoundrel. So here's your opportunity, Mom. Unless you're very careful you're going to get caught. If you can recognize the blackmail for what it is, though, before long you'll be able to resist the urge to be a hero.

Both Allen and I have always told the girls that "my home is your home . . . anytime." They always knew that no matter which of us they were living with, they could visit the other. We operated on the premise that children need both of their parents.

One day Jennifer, a high school senior by then, called to say she wanted to come be with me. "I'm coming home, Mom," she announced. "I can't stand this place any more. This woman is driving me crazy. I hate it here, and I'm coming home. All my life you've said I could come home when I wanted to. Well I want to now."

It took some time, but finally I was able to discover the reason she wanted to run. She and Sue were having problems.

"Jennifer, you're absolutely right. You *can* come home, just as soon as you fix up that relationship with Sue."

"But Mom, you said anytime . . ."

"Honey, you *can* come home as soon as you straighten things out with Sue. But you're not going to run to my house because you've got a rotten relationship. You can't just walk away from that problem."

She *did* get the problem with Sue straightened out, and she didn't come home. She didn't need to.

Jennifer might still be nursing that poor relationship with Sue if I had said, "Of course, dear. If that nasty woman isn't treating you right, come home to Mom. I'll take good care of you."

The reality of the situation was that their dad was married to Sue. They needed a relationship with him, and that meant relating to Sue. Whether I liked the idea or not, their relationship with their dad and with Sue needed to be a good one.

Gifts

Watch out. Here's another temptation to play super-parent. The role can be an exciting one; the rewards are immediate. But the long-term results can be devastating.

Buying children the world will not buy their affection and loyalty. You can never make up for all the "wrongs" of the other parent in a weekend.

With our girls, all weekend long I tried to be a super-parent. I was always taking them to bigger and better places, buying them bigger and better things. They had everything money could buy.

Both Allen and I had been caught in the gift-buying trap, without realizing it. When Allen bought Jennifer an electric typewriter for her graduation—from sixth grade—I said, "Isn't that a bit much?" We both laughed and agreed that it was. We began telling each other what we were going to buy for the girls and felt free to help keep each other's gifts at a more realistic level.

What the children do need from each parent is *quality time*. There is no substitute for that, and it isn't a drain on the budget.

The Children's "Things"

Let the children keep some of their things at each house. That way they can feel more at home in either place. The parent that has custody has a natural tendency to want *that* home to be "home." The children only *visit* the other home. But that's not good for the children. Either home should look like children live there.

Older Children

Older young people do indeed feel the changes brought on by divorce. Don't make the mistake of assuming they know what's going on and will understand. From "children" in their twenties you may get the message, "I want to get away from here." Don't read this as alienation due to the divorce. Talk with them honestly about what has happened. But when you get the "I-want-to-get-away" message, recognize that this is a feeling of virtually *every* young person in their twenties. Don't blame it on the divorce . . . and on yourself.

Stepchildren

The biggest mistake a stepparent can make is to try to be a parent to the stepchild. This is especially true if the absent natural parent is still active in the child's life.

The most you can give the child is friendship. And remember, with children you earn the right to be a friend. Many people operate on the basis that an adult need only announce his or her arrival and say, "I'm going to be your friend" in order to become a child's friend. *Not so fast.*

Stepparents are automatically treated with suspicion just because they're new. Then, to the extent that you try to be a parent, you will be treated with resentment because you are seen as trying to usurp the place of the natural parent.

Conflicts arising out of stepparenting are a major destroyer of second marriages. Show a lot of patience. Don't make a cause out of winning a stepchild's love. Remember that in relationships, trying to make something happen often has the opposite effect.

If the stepchildren are old enough, it may be necessary for them to move away from home in order for the new marriage to be preserved.

Loyal to Whom?

At the risk of saying it too often, I want to make this point one more time: Children need *both* parents. To the extent that it is possible, this means letting them feel comfortable with each parent.

This also means learning not to put down your ex-mate in front of the children. Constantly reminding your children of your ex-mate's faults gives you a temporary sense of satisfaction. But several destructive things happen in the process. First, your child knows he is half of that ex-mate. If his dad is a no-good, low-down scoundrel, it must follow in your child's mind that he is a half of a no-good, low-down scoundrel. Without meaning to, you've just told him that.

Secondly, when your child gets a little older, wiser, and more discerning, he or she is going to discover that that ex-mate is not really the completely no-good, low-down scoundrel you described. That realization creates a barrier between you and your child.

This happens very often. Frequently, a mother will say to me, "My son is grown now, and he's always over visiting his dad. I can't understand it. For years I told him what his dad is like. Now he won't come to see me, but he's always at his dad's."

As the child matured, he had no alternative but to believe that his mother must have lied to him. *She's* responsible for robbing him of the relationship he might have had with his father all these years.

Especially in the time just after my first divorce, the hostility I felt towards Allen was always just below the surface, ready to explode. I was bitter, and he deserved to know it. Some days just thinking about the divorce for a few moments made me feel as if I had had a drink of sulphuric acid for breakfast. Then, whenever I had a chance, I would spit it out at whomever was around. But I managed to keep that from the girls. Both Allen and I tried very hard not to tell the girls that the other was a rotten person, or to let anyone else say that in their presence.

When, in the process of picking up the girls, I couldn't avoid Allen, our conversations were quite mechanical and very proper. I always managed to keep from blowing up until we were on the phone.

"Pumping" the Kids

No matter how desperately you want to know what's going on with your ex-mate, *don't pump the kids for information.*

Often when I went to pick up the girls on the weekend, Mrs. Alderssmith, Allen's housekeeper, would tell me all that had happened during the week. I listened to all the details. I knew who Allen was dating, what he was doing, and where he was going. I had a *need* to know that. The truth was I had never divorced myself from him. I had signed papers that *said* I was divorced, but deep inside I was still married. He was mine, and I was his. I had a right to know what he was doing.

When Mrs. Alderssmith wasn't available I would pump the girls for information. They were almost always full of stories to tell, and I knew how to get the information I wanted to hear.

"Sue was there," they would report. I never asked direct, obvious questions. Instead I used, "Well, I suppose Sue feels they shouldn't do that."

"No, I don't think so, Mom. She said . . ." And I found out what I wanted to know.

Before Allen and Sue were married, if I wanted to know if she was at his apartment I might use, "I bet it was great to spend that time alone with your dad."

"Actually, we weren't alone with him. Sue was there."

"Well, at least you got to spend some time with him."

"Oh, yeah! She went home in the afternoon."

When I would use some of that information against Allen, he would accuse me of pumping the girls.

"Not me!" I responded self-righteously. "They're very open with me. They tell me everything." (Everything I could squeeze out of them!)

You see what was happening, don't you? I was still keeping my ex-marriage very much alive, feeding it regularly with morsels of information I had no need to know. In the process, I was turning innocent children into spies. And that has to be destructive.

Visitation

The whole business of visitation was another problem area we sought to solve in a way that was least damaging to the girls.

"I think it is more appropriate for the girls to live with you right now. My work is so hectic," I remember saying to Allen. Other times Allen would say to me, "You know, I'm working twenty-four hours a day, seven days a week right now. I'm not able to spend much time with the girls. What are your circumstances? Maybe they ought to live with you." Most of the time we were able to separate their welfare from our personal feelings of animosity for each other.

Holidays

Through all the anger and pain, neither of us put the girls in the position of having to make a choice as to which one they loved the most, or which one they wanted to live with. We never asked them where they wanted to spend Thanksgiving or Christmas. We *told* them where they were going.

"You're going to spend Christmas with your dad until noon. I'll pick you up then."

Even though it sometimes was painful, we really tried to figure out what was best for them.

Keeping the Visitation Schedule

Try to set mutually agreeable times, *and stick by them*. The emotions of both ex-mates are especially high when picking up or returning a child. Be sensitive to that. Don't use those times to punish your ex-mate. Stick to your agreements, and you will reduce the strain in an already difficult situation.

Family

Families sometimes do strange things in a divorce. A mother may blame her daughter rather than her son-in-law. Families tend to polarize, and more often than not they do not divide along bloodlines.

When you are desperately looking for support and validation, it's easy to feel that support from your ex-mate's family is a special victory. If they see him or her as bad, they must be right.

Don't soak up that support. Let the families, and especially the children's grandparents, know that each of them still means a great deal to you (if they really do) and that you want to maintain those relationships as much as possible. Especially encourage the children to keep a relationship with their grandparents. Try to see them as special, important people in their own rights, even though the relationship that brought you together has been dissolved.

Friends

Friends almost always take sides in a divorce, or they disappear.

When you tell them you're divorcing, some will respond, "Good for you. I never did like what he was doing to you. You're better off without him."

They're trying to be supportive, working hard to make you feel better. You want to be able to talk about your ex-mate, but you don't want someone else to do it. When they berate him it diminishes you. You feel betrayed and your relationship with your friend is strained, just at the time when you most need friends.

When you feel this kind of problem developing, it's best to be direct with your friends if you can. Explain that your feelings are all confused right now. Tell them how you feel when they criticize your ex-mate. Let them know how much you need their love and understanding. Your true friends will understand and try to cooperate.

"No man is an island. No man stands alone," the poet

John Donne wrote. At no time in your life is that so true as at the time of divorce. When much about your life is painful, unattractive, and tends to drive people away, try to go quietly and gently among family and friends, finding strength in a few caring, healing relationships you choose to maintain. They can help you find the strength you need to work through the relationships you cannot escape.

CHAPTER 17

Sex and Singleness

Lots of very pious things are said about the subject of dating. In order not to speak from too lofty a pinnacle, I have chosen to take you on a guided tour of my own experience in the world of dating. Maybe you can look at it as a kind of diary, with footnotes that may make some of the lessons I've learned a little clearer and more helpful.

* * *

For years after my second divorce, I tried very hard to feel contented as a single person. But it never really worked. After all, I hadn't really chosen singleness. I had chosen divorce, and singleness was the result of my action. It wasn't really what I had wanted.

Friends talked about how much I had grown since the divorce and how I was well on the way to becoming a "fulfilled woman." But they weren't talking about arriving at some place of inner peace. They were talking about another marriage. In their minds *I was half of a whole.*

Worse still, despite all my efforts at singleness, my insides told me the same thing. Fulfillment *did* mean finding somebody. My friends were right, I thought.

Back in the Dating Business

I think it's foolish for people to say, "I'm not going to date. You won't catch me going out until I find the right person."

The very idea of dating sounds both fun and frightening, probably more frightening than fun. New relationships, especially male-female relationships, can be uncomfortable. So long as you were married, you knew pretty much what to expect when you went out. The restaurants you went to, the food you ate, the things you did—everything fit into a comfortable pattern.

The idea of being a charming listener, of doing new things that you may not like, wondering whether or not your date likes you—of course it's frightening. But think for a moment how good it feels to have a thoughtful companion. Think of the good feeling of being admired by someone of the opposite sex. That's the pleasant side of dating, and I highly recommend it. Once I decided to go out, dates weren't hard to get.

Very early I realized that Prince Charming wasn't going to break down my door to find me. So I got out where the people were—church activities, social functions, and gatherings of all kinds. Night after night I had invitations. And night after night I went out with different men. If I was going to find my Prince Charming, I had to look, didn't I?

I even went out with men I didn't want to go out with. When they asked for dates, I didn't know how to say no, or maybe I was *afraid* to hurt their feelings. I was even more afraid of what a no would do to my image as a "nice person."

Some of those dates were painful, uncomfortable evenings. I died inside a hundred times. I wished I was at home. And for every bit of pain I felt, every escape wish I made on those dates, I'm sure my date felt more pain and wished more wishes.

Yet I let it happen time and time again, not even realizing what I was doing. Soon I found myself trying to get out of dates I didn't want to keep. I lied about my schedule or hinted that I had a terminal illness and couldn't possibly be well by Saturday.

Finally I had to face the stark reality that once again I was a failure where men were concerned. I was blowing it. "And," I thought to myself, "just when things were going so well. Just when I thought I was really growing."

Days later I was still looking for a way to say no, a way I could live with. Over coffee one afternoon, a young student who was working as a computer programmer suggested, "Pat, just say, 'Thank you for asking, but I'd rather not.' That way a man isn't offended. He doesn't feel put down. And you've said no."

"Aarggh! I can't do that. What if he says . . . or what if he does . . . I can't do that. It sounds awful." I paused for a moment, then spilled out my *real* fear. "He won't like me anymore."

"Do you really want him to like you *that* way, Pat?" he asked in frustration. "Wouldn't you prefer that he respect your honesty? Don't you want him to quit pressuring you for dates? Don't you want him to know once and for all that no matter what he thinks he is picking up from you, you are not interested? Isn't that what you want?"

I took the suggestion, and it worked. I was able to say no. But why did these men think I was interested in them? Where did they get the message? The answers to those questions didn't make me feel good.

I often still felt insecure in my relationships with men. I wanted very much to be loved and accepted, and I wanted to be loving and accepting. I didn't know how to convey that message without it also being an unspoken invitation to get closer. Even when I didn't want to convey that message at all, that's what was coming across. I had developed a way of dealing with men that couldn't be turned on and off like a faucet.

Discovering Body Language

I had never thought of myself as a sexy woman. I liked people—men *and* women. For years I had been cold and calculating in my relationships. Now, because God's love had warmed my heart, I was learning to reach out in friendship and caring.

But time after time my caring was being misread. At first I decided it was the fault of the men I dated. It had to be them.

Then a Christian counselor caught me up short. "Pat, you are sexually attractive to men."

Men had told me that, but I had dismissed it as a prelude to intimacy. Now the doctor was saying it, and I had to listen. With her help, I saw what I was doing. For openers, I realized that I was a very "touching" person. I would come up to a man and smile and start talking.

Because I talk with my hands, I would end up touching him throughout the conversation—putting my hand on his arm or shoulder in the process of making my point.

I learned to stop doing that, or at least to do it only when I choose to relate to a man more intimately.

Psychologists say everyone has a pre-defined "space" around them, a kind of protective area. For most people it is about two feet wide. My tendency was to stand close to a man. I discovered that by doing so I was unconsciously saying I wanted to be intimate. So I learned to keep a comfortable space between myself and a man (unless, of course, I wanted to be more intimate).

I love to have guests for dinner. It seemed natural to invite a man whose company I enjoyed. But men seemed to read into my invitation something more intimate than I intended. Solution: Make the dinner gracious and lovely, but keep the lights up and the drapes open.

Just Friends

Somewhere in my often impatient adjustment to singleness, I learned that as long as you're single *and still looking*, singleness is a very insecure feeling.

I was a frequent victim of the "Saturday-night syndrome." I had to have a date *every* Saturday night. Whether I did or not became a test of my worth. With no Saturday night date I felt insecure. I must be undesirable. Could it be I was losing my touch? But give me a Saturday night date and everything was fine.

The rule seemed to be: Be desirable at all costs.

Eventually I developed the ability to consider a date as an enjoyable evening that didn't necessarily have to be even remotely related to the possibility of marriage. As a result, I have dated men I would never consider marrying, and many of those dates have been pleasant surprises.

To date only men you might want to marry is to place an undue strain on the date and the relationship. You're too busy evaluating your prospect and too concerned about his response to you to relax and enjoy the date.

But what about a second, third, or fourth date? Isn't that an automatic indication that the relationship is getting "serious"? Absolutely not. I think the idea that a man and a woman cannot have a continuing relationship that is not romantic is *pure myth*. Open, honest, friendly relationships *are* possible—and very enjoyable. A man does not have to attract you physically or "turn you on" to be good company, share common interests, and add a special non-threatening joy to your life.

If you have that kind of a relationship, guard it. If you don't, don't automatically reject the possibility.

Games Divorced People Play

By nature most of us are game players. We've developed the skill so carefully that we no longer recognize the games we play.

What do I mean by a "game"? How do I know when I'm playing one? For me, game-playing simply means my efforts to get you to do something I want you to do: pure and simple *manipulation*.

When I'm playing a game, I feel frustrated because you're not doing what I have worked to get you to do. Or, when you finally do it, I sense a hollow victory rather than feeling genuinely satisfied.

Women often manipulate men into taking them out to dinner. This is called "the steak date." You're not interested in the man, but you do have to be able to report to the girls that you went to a lovely place for dinner over the weekend. So you manipulate any man into inviting you, and you make sure it's a very nice place. You do that by talking rich, by letting him know in lots of little ways that you "*never* eat at this place or that."

Women also play a game I call "by no means maybe." That game is meant to put the responsibility for sex on the man. "After all, I *said* no! But he went ahead anyway."

Men have their games, too. One of them is not believing that their advances could possibly be turned down.

One lawyer—an attractive guy—asked me for a date. I'd known him for some time through a social group at the church. We'd been casual but good friends. We had a great time, except for one thing. He couldn't keep his hands off me. I tried very hard to be nice, but I was constantly backing off, constantly taking his hands off my body.

Some time during the evening he invited me out again for the next Saturday night.

At the end of that first date I invited him in. There was a light in his eye as he accepted my invitation. But I had something else in mind.

"Sit down for a minute," I almost ordered him. "Look, Paul, I really like you a lot, and I want to see you again. But I have to tell you that I am very uncomfortable when you have your hands all over me. We don't know each other well enough to be that familiar. And besides, I just don't like it."

"Pat, I'm sorry. I'm just a very warm person. If that makes you uncomfortable, I won't do it any more. I want you to be comfortable with me. *Please* forgive me. It won't happen again."

I felt the air was cleared and we understood each other. But the next date was the same thing all over again, and I don't think he ever really understood why I quit dating him. He just couldn't believe I meant what I said.

Sex

For a long time, I thought part of being desirable included sex. I knew deep inside that it wasn't *supposed* to include sex. Often I was troubled by my sexual involvements, but not enough to say no all the time.

Let me share my battle with you.

The Bible says no very clearly. But that wasn't enough for me. I wanted to argue.

"Why should I say no? Come on, Lord. It's part of life, part of the way You made us. Besides," I was mustering my biggest argument now, "most of my Christian single friends are hopping into bed regularly."

"You must turn Your head for single people, don't You? I know I'm not supposed to mess around with *married* men. That's adultery. And if I were married, I wouldn't fool around on my husband. That's adultery, too. But I'm a single, red-blooded American woman. What am I supposed to do about that? Surely those old rules don't apply to people in *my* position.

"And besides, Lord, I'm not promiscuous. I'm very selective about the men I go to bed with. And I don't do it as often as most of the women I know."

I'd given the battle my best shot. But it wasn't enough.

In the weeks that followed I often thought back over my sexual experiences. I remembered the excitement, the thrill, and even some funny experiences. Yet as I relived those times, something began to dawn on me. The more I gave in to my sexual urges, the less satisfied I felt.

"Come on," I argued with myself. "That can't be true." But it was. There wasn't any escaping that fact.

I realized that with each new sexual experience, something was happening to my self-esteem. The fun and excitement were there, but afterwards I felt uncomfortable. It hadn't been *that* good. Something was missing, and no amount of virtuous activity could seem to put back what I had given up.

There was something else, too. I began to see that my sex partner and I seldom *really* got to know each other. Our time together wasn't helping us learn about one another, and it wasn't enough just to enjoy one another. Instead, the sexual thing put a constraint on building any *real* relationship. Despite what I wanted to believe, the facts were simple: Everything focused on getting *my* needs met.

"O.K., O.K." my insides said. "That's enough."

I hadn't counted on God cutting off that part of my fun.

"Lord, I'm a liberated woman." I had to make one last-ditch effort.

"Yes, but are you liberated enough to say no?" my thoughts echoed back.

"O.K., O.K., You win." It had taken weeks to come to that point. "But abstinence is no fun. How do I do it? I'm bombarded by temptation. It's all around. And besides, sometimes this body demands attention when I least expect it."

The first step, I found, was to stop kidding myself into believing that sex was okay for single people. Once I was able to admit that sexual activity was an act of disobedience to God, I began to see the consequences more clearly.

For openers, my personality deteriorated. It wasn't something that happened right away, but it *did* happen. I saw it in other people, and I'm sure they could see it in me. There is a hardness in the lives of people who go from one affair to the next. There is a kind of hostility toward life that runs deep underneath the best of public manners. Under their mask of gaiety is the evidence of inner turmoil.

I saw it in *them*. Then I saw it in my own mirror, and I didn't want what I saw.

"How can I ever make it, Lord? I'm so weak. I need so much love. Can I ever make 'no sex' stick?"

In the Scriptures I read about Joseph in Potiphar's house. I got the message: Control your circumstances as much as you can. Learn to sense when things are getting out of control. Then be ready to run. Get away from situations where sexual drives cannot be controlled.

"Sounds hard, Lord. I'll have to have Your help." And time and time again He *has* helped.

It took a while for me to settle the no-sex question. The

conclusion should have been obvious, I suppose, but it wasn't. No one in the church dealt with the whole area of sex in a loving, caring way. It was either "Thou shalt not," with never a practical suggestion on *how* thou shalt not, or a rationalization by Christian friends as to why sex was okay for singles.

Many of my friends, critical of my position, accused me of having "sexual hangups." Some even suggested I had become frigid.

When "No" Means "Maybe"

Everywhere you turn, sex is more open these days.

Many women tell me they have phone calls from casual acquaintances asking if they'd like to have sexual relations. No invitation to dinner, not even, "Let's go to the movies"—just plain, "Let's have sex."

It used to be a common, though not publicly accepted practice, to hire a prostitute. Then, as sex became more available, the price became a nice dinner. After all, the man had paid for the privilege, and sex was just a way to repay the favor.

But things have changed again. Now they've done away with dinner.

This is a special problem for divorced women. Many men feel that a divorced woman is so sexually starved that she must be panting for sex. The suggestion makes me angry. Sure, I have sexual needs, but I am not available.

Many men do not take no for an answer. Why is that? When I put that question to some men I could talk to about such things, the answer was always the same. "Because most women *mean* maybe, no matter what they say."

I've checked it out with the women, and the men are right. The women *do* mean maybe. They say no because they feel that is expected. They're nice girls, and nice girls say no. But they're hoping that the men won't accept that. It's a case of, "I've said what I'm supposed to. Now let's get on with the hanky-panky."

What If We're Getting Married?

In the process of trying to learn sexual obedience, I discovered something else. Men talk about marriage very early in a relationship. For some divorced men it seems to be, "I don't have time for all this courtship business. I've been down this road before. I know what I want. Let's get on with it." A gal who is looking for another husband can find herself in a new marriage before she realizes what has happened to her.

For other men, I'm convinced the marriage talk early in a relationship is a prelude to going to bed.

Even the single people who have the strongest feelings against premarital sex seem to feel it is all right if you are talking about marriage. So if you go out with a girl on the first date and she turns you on, on the second date you start talking about marriage. Then on the third date you go to bed together. The marriage talk makes it proper.

I've had some of the most incredible proposals you can imagine. A man who didn't even know my middle name asked me to marry him. At first the proposals were kind of flattering. Then I realized they weren't proposals meant to end in marriage. They were simply meant to end in bed.

Maybe these men really *thought* that they wanted to get married. But underneath it all was a hunger for companionship . . . and sex.

It's Not All the Man's Fault

For a woman, sex is in the head, and for a man it's more biological. Many women act as if men and women both operate on the same sexual schedule, that both pass the turn-on point at the same time. That just isn't so. Men usually are turned on much earlier than women.

Physical intimacy is a very satisfying thing. A man reaches for a woman's hand. Without saying a word, she signals whether or not that's acceptable. Then he may touch her shoulder or some other part of her body, and again she signals approval.

Everything is very lovely, very flattering up to this point. But ladies, if you continue petting to the point where you are turned on sexually, the man is most likely at or very near the point of no return. I don't take *all* the responsibility for sexual abstinence, but I do take a big chunk of the responsibility. Basically, I stop before my date becomes aroused.

Masturbation

Nowhere in the Bible is there a direct commandment against masturbation. But for most people, masturbation requires a very active fantasy. A person imagines that he or she is having sexual relations with a member of the opposite sex. What is happening is that he or she is meeting his physical/sexual needs *all alone*. Something beautiful, something that is meant to be a close, physically intimate experience has been made into a solo performance.

I do not want to lay down some kind of rule for everyone on this matter. But although masturbation does not seem to be expressly forbidden in Scripture and it does relieve sexual pressures without marring your life and the life of another, remember that practical problems develop when you must concoct and sustain an active fantasy in order to reach a climax.

One Final Word

In the beginning, God made man and woman to need each other. "It is not good for man to be alone," God said when he brought the woman to the man.

Something deep within us echoes that first statement about human relationships. We long for intimacy. Yet we risk destroying something of ourselves and something beautiful in another person if we pursue sexual intimacy.

Don't be lured into the "logic" that says, "God has a different standard for divorced people." Nothing but convenient rationalization supports that idea.

"Trust in the LORD, and do good; Dwell in the land and cultivate faithfulness. Delight yourself in the LORD; And he will give you the desires of your heart. Commit your way to the LORD, Trust also in Him and He will do it" (Ps. 37:3,4, NASB).

EPILOGUE

Let me bring you up to date. I'm forty-four now. And it feels good. I haven't "arrived" anywhere, but I *am* a becomer. In retrospect I can actually say, "Thank You, Lord, for the pain, the lessons, the learning, and the growing. A lot of years and a generous amount of Your love and forgiveness have gone into bringing me to this place."

I'm five-foot-five, have brown hair, brown eyes, and I'm single. It's easier now to say that than it used to be. However, my singleness is only one of the many circumstances of my life. It is no more than that—one more descriptive statement. In no way does it define who I am, any more than my height or my age define who I am.

Many of my friends are married. Many others are single women, and some are single men. I'm learning to relate to men more easily these days.

I can see many evidences of growth in my life. After all these years, it turns out that wisdom and discernment are *really* ours for the asking. They're gifts from God.

There's no more need to grasp at loving, not so much need to hold on to people when they want to let go. I *am* loved. God loves me. I find that satisfying and fulfilling. The deeper level of commitment I've been able to make to a chaste life helps when temptations come—and they do come occasionally, even now.

Karen is twenty-one and married. She's in college and working. And she is my good friend. She has little need for my maternal advice, but we still share experiences and a lot of love.

Jennifer is twenty-three, and she, too, is married. She's teaching, having graduated from a university and she, like Karen, is a good friend. In many ways she is my spiritual advisor—an ever-present help who encourages and loves me.

Allen and Sue are married. Our relationship is relaxed, yet honest and supportive, even though we don't see each other socially. I love little Mike, their four-year-old son. "How is it, Lord, that he can be Jennifer and Karen's little brother and not be related to me?" So, I pretend that he is. I practice "grandmothering" on him in preparation for the time when I will really be one.

And Jim, dear Jim, hasn't changed much. He could never seem to accept our divorce. It seems hard for him to imagine that I would choose not to go back to him and all those "things." For many years he was sure that I would cease to be a religious fanatic, give up this whole Christian nonsense, come to my senses, and remarry him. For six or seven years we had dinner together fairly regularly. I tried very hard to explain my new moral standards. I wanted to introduce him to my new Lord, and I tried praying him into God's family. But it only irritated him. "I liked you better the way you were before, Pat. You've changed, and I don't like it."

He, too, remarried, finally. The last time he called I wished him God's blessings, and I told him that I hoped he would be truly happy with his new wife and be good to her. He cried.

Love is strange. I've learned that. I'm still learning it. You can love, and not be in love. You can love and hate at the same time. You can do the loving thing without "feeling" anything.

My relationship to God is more open now than it has been. He continues to ask me, "Pat, what is your motive?" My answer isn't always right. That's an area of continued growth for me. And I suspect He'll keep on asking that same question.

I trust my answer will continue to be an honest, growing one.

I'm glad to be growing, even when the growing gets tough. Life began for me years ago in a little village in New Mexico. And time and again it has seemed to stop. Life began again in Las Vegas. God's love reached out to a woman who thought she was unlovable. And that magnificent love has helped to shape a whole new life for me—a life that will never stop.

I've picked up some of the broken pieces of my life and put them back into place. But there have been other pieces, too badly broken, too scarred by the traumas I've faced to ever be repaired. And yet the master Potter, the Lord of broken lives, has put those pieces into place in ways I could never have imagined.

Today the process still goes on, as He shapes a life according to His design. And the more I discover of His plan, the more deeply fulfilling, the more exciting, the more wonder-filled my life becomes. . . . He has turned, and continually keeps on turning, my disasters into a *grand adventure*.

Summer, 1979